The Nuclear Waste Primer

A Handbook for Citizens

▼

The League of Women Voters Education Fund

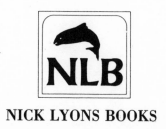

NICK LYONS BOOKS

Manufactured in the United States of America

10 9 8 7 6 5 4 3 2 1

Library of Congress Cataloging-in-Publication Data
Main entry under title:

The Nuclear waste primer.

  Bibliography: p.
  1. Radioactive waste disposal—United States.
I. League of Women Voters (U.S.). Education Fund.
TD898.N834 1985   363.7'28   85–19880
ISBN0–8052–6007–2
ISBN 0–8052–6006–4 (pbk.)

ISBN: 0-8052-6007-2 (cloth); 0-8052-6006-4 (paperback)

Contents

Preface

Preface

The aim of this publication is to offer the nonexpert a concise, balanced introduction to nuclear waste. It outlines the dimensions of the problem, discussing the types and quantities of waste. It then defines the sources, types, and hazards of radiation and reviews the history, major laws, and current status of both high level and low level waste management. Finally, it describes how citizens can plug into nuclear waste decision-making and identifies selected information sources.

The authors of *The Nuclear Waste Primer* are Isabelle P. Weber, Natural Resources Director, League of Women Voters Education Fund, and Susan D. Wiltshire, J.K. Associates, South Hamilton, Massachusetts. (The predecessor publication was written by Marjorie Beane, Director of the Nuclear Energy Education Program, League of Women Voters Education Fund.) The authors are indebted to Diane Greer, Administrative Assistant, who prepared countless drafts of the primer. The LWVEF also acknowledges with appreciation the contributions made by the many reviewers of the draft manuscript.

1

Introduction to the Issues

▼   ▼   ▼   ▼   ▼

How large is the problem of radioactive waste? One way to gauge its scale is to tally up how much already has been generated. As of 1983 the total included:

roughly 306,000 cubic meters of high-level wastes (mostly liquid) from defense programs, nearly all located at government facilities;

4,626 cubic meters of highly radioactive spent (used) fuel rods from nuclear reactors, most of which are stored at nuclear power plants;

3,080,000 cubic meters of low-level radioactive wastes (contaminated work gloves, tools, medical isotopes, irradiated reactor components, and the like), permanently disposed of at both government and commercial facilities;

96,500,000 cubic meters of radioactive tailings from active uranium mining and processing, almost all located in sparsely populated regions in Arizona, New Mexico, Utah, and Wyoming.

These radioactive wastes are the result, mainly, of the successive steps in the production of nuclear weapons and in the generation

1

of electricity from fission reactors. The types differ significantly in their physical form and in the intensity and nature of the radiation they emit. The most potentially dangerous high-level wastes (see below) come from both weapons manufacture and from the reprocessing of spent fuel rods to salvage unused fuel elements. At present, since no reprocessing of spent fuel rods from commercial reactors is taking place, these rods have to be dealt with as if they, too, were high-level waste and must be stored in a way that protects people and the environment from the high levels of penetrating radiation they emit. The low-level wastes and the tailings require quite different procedures for disposal.

Management of these wastes received relatively little attention from policymakers in the first three decades of the nuclear era (1945–1975). During that time, scientists and regulators and promoters of nuclear power tended to view waste management as a technical problem for which modern technology would provide a solution. Wastes were treated, stored, or disposed of with an eye toward convenient, short-term solutions—solutions that unfortunately created new waste-disposal problems. The federal government spent billions of dollars to produce nuclear weapons and later to commercialize nuclear power in the 1950s and 1960s; only $300 million was spent during the same period to research processes to solidify liquid high-level wastes and to isolate them in geologic formations.

It was not until the late 1970s that the federal government allocated substantial funds and personnel to develop a plan for the long-term management of nuclear wastes.

By 1980 the critical necessity to find a permanent solution to managing nuclear wastes became abundantly clear for several reasons:

There were only three commercial operating low-level waste-disposal sites—Barnwell, South Carolina; Beatty, Nevada; and Hanford, Washington—to serve nuclear power plants, medical and research facilities, and other industries. And governors in those states had given notice that they planned to cut back on the amount of low-level waste their facilities would accept in the future. South Carolina's governor had refused to take any of the low-level waste generated by the March 1979 accident at Three Mile Island.

Since spent fuel rods were not being reprocessed, the inventories of spent fuel kept in storage pools at nuclear power plants were growing, and some pools were filling up. Unless utilities could gain state and federal approval to increase the capacity of existing facilities, to build additional pools, or to ship spent fuel to unfilled basins at other reactors—or unless the federal government provided interim storage facilities—several power plants faced the prospect of serious storage problems by the late 1980s and possible shutdown in the mid-1990s.

The future of nuclear power was at stake. There was a growing public skepticism that methods and materials to contain radioactive wastes could endure over the very long time required for nuclear waste to decay. In the late 1970s several states passed laws prohibiting further nuclear power plant construction until the federal government demonstrated that the waste could be disposed of safely and permanently. Other states restricted or prohibited the storage and disposal of radioactive wastes, of whatever radiation level, within their borders.

News of radioactive wastes leaking from government storage tanks and of the dispersal of abandoned uranium mill tailings in the environment added to the public's fears and distrust of the federal government's ability to develop and carry out a waste-management system that would provide adequate safeguards for both public health and the environment.

Figure 1. Nuclear power plants in the United States as of July 1, 1985. *Atomic Industrial Forum, Inc.*

Key
● Reactors With Operating License
○ Reactors With Construction Permit
△ Reactors On Order

94	Reactors operable*........................	80,095 MWe
33	Reactors with construction permits	36,486 MWe
2	Reactors on order.........................	2,240 MWe
129	Total....................................	118,821 MWe

*Also shown on the map are two reactors with operating licenses which have been shut down: Three Mile Island 1 — 819 MWe; Three Mile Island 2 — 906 MWe.

Nuclear proponents and foes alike called for nuclear waste-management decisions the nation could, literally, live with. The debate brought to the surface a number of basic questions. What kinds of institutional mechanisms do we need to assure the total isolation of radioactive wastes from the environment for the long periods required to render them harmless? How much safety should we require in the transportation, handling, and storage of nuclear wastes? Will the federal government deal fairly with the states in the selection and development of high-level waste-disposal sites? How can the federal government overcome the past legacy of distrust and problems that feed the "not-in-my-backyard" syndrome?

It was against this background that Congress, in the late 1970s, began considering comprehensive radioactive waste legislation. After a number of false starts, Congress passed two major pieces of legislation—the Low-Level Radioactive Waste Policy Act of 1980 and the Nuclear Waste Policy Act of 1982 (both discussed in Chapter 5). Together these laws provide the framework for resolving the key questions related to the management of low-level and high-level waste, a framework that was lacking in previous federal waste-management efforts. These laws do not, however, provide answers to all the scientific and technical questions—or to the potentially more difficult social, political, and institutional questions. These are questions that not just scientists but also citizens and public officials must help to answer.

Both the Low-Level Radioactive Waste Policy Act and the Nuclear Waste Policy Act acknowledge the important part that state and local governments, policymakers, and individual citizens must play in making these complex policy decisions. But it will take the goodwill and best efforts of all the players to make this process work. The challenge to our society is to find ways within the framework of our federal form of government to develop a nuclear waste disposal system that is technically sound and politically and socially acceptable.

WHO'S IN CHARGE?

Department of Energy (DOE)   Formed in 1977, the Department of Energy absorbed from its predecessor agencies, the Atomic Energy Commission (AEC, 1946–1974) and the Energy Research and Development Administration (ERDA, 1974–1977), the responsibility for nuclear research and development, including waste management. DOE has the overall assignment of carrying out the federal government's high-level waste-management policies. In addition, it is responsible for national planning and coordination with states and other entities in the development of a national low-level waste-management and -disposal system.

DOE's Office of Civilian Radioactive Waste Management is the lead office for the development and construction of one or more geologic repositories for disposal of spent fuel and high-level waste generated in commercial nuclear programs and for the operation of the waste-management system (which must be licensed by the Nuclear Regulatory Commission). In addition, other offices in DOE are in charge of handling inactive uranium-mill tailing sites and transuranic and low-level waste generated by defense nuclear programs.

Environmental Protection Agency (EPA) Established in 1970, the Environmental Protection Agency is charged with providing federal guidance for all radiation directly or indirectly affecting public health and the environment and with setting generally applicable environmental standards. Thus, EPA is responsible for developing environmental-protection criteria for the handling and disposal of all radioactive wastes. The agency has issued proposed standards for high-level waste disposal in geologic repositories and for the land disposal of low-level waste; final standards are expected to be promulgated in late 1985. The Uranium Mill Tailings Radiation Control Act of 1978 requires EPA to establish environmental standards for uranium mill sites.

Nuclear Regulatory Commission (NRC) Established in 1974, the Nuclear Regulatory Commission is an independent regulatory agency. The NRC develops and enforces regulations to protect the public health and safety from all commercial nuclear activities, including active uranium-mill tailing sites. It licenses and regulates commercial power plants, industries, individuals, and organizations that possess and use radioactive materials. NRC shares with the Department of Transportation the responsibility for developing, regulating, and enforcing safety standards for the transportation of radioactive waste.

NRC has issued regulations (based on anticipated EPA standards) for a mined geologic repository and also has published regulations covering the land disposal of low-level waste.

Department of Transportation (DOT)   The Department of Transportation regulates the shipment of all privately owned radioactive materials, including nuclear waste, by all modes of transport. DOT is responsible for labeling, classification, and marking of all radioactive waste packages.

U.S. Geological Survey (USGS)   The U.S. Geological Survey, in the Department of the Interior, serves as technical advisor to the Department of Energy and the Nuclear Regulatory Commission. It conducts geologic investigations in support of DOE's high-level waste-disposal programs, including providing data for DOE's use in environmental assessments of potential high-level waste-disposal sites. The USGS also has conducted geologic and hydrologic investigations on existing low-level waste sites and will act as a consultant to NRC when the commission considers DOE applications for high-level waste-disposal facilities.

Bureau of Land Management (BLM)   The Bureau of Land Management, also in the Department of the Interior, reviews environmental assessments, environmental impact statements, land acquisitions procedures, and any other plans to site waste-disposal facilities on federal lands over which it has jurisdiction.

2

Sources

▼　　　▼　　　▼　　　▼　　　▼

Where do radioactive wastes come from? The dialogue about nuclear waste management would be a lot easier to conduct if we could talk about a single activity and a uniform kind of waste material. But it is not that simple.

It all starts with radioactive atoms, known as radioisotopes, that are energetically unstable; that is, they have too much energy. Radioisotopes become more stable by giving up some of this extra radiation energy—in the form of either particles or rays—through a process called radioactive decay. Some radioisotopes occur in nature, and we put some of these to use in what are now routine ways. For example, we use uranium as a reactor fuel and naturally occurring radioactive carbon for dating archeological artifacts. Some naturally radioactive materials eventually find their way into the nuclear waste stream. But the bulk of the most potentially dangerous nuclear waste is composed of the fission products that are produced in a nuclear reactor.

From World War II until the present time, U.S. defense activities have generated the greatest volume of nuclear wastes. However, even though the wastes (primarily spent fuel) from the commercial sector are now only a small fraction of the volume resulting from defense programs, they are more radioactive because they have had less time to decay and are in a more concentrated form. By the end of the century, commercial wastes, including spent fuel assemblies, will greatly exceed defense wastes in radiation content (see Figure 2).

TYPES OF WASTE

Radioactive wastes are differentiated by the *intensity* of their radiation—that is, by the number of "rays" or particles emitted per second per unit of volume. They also differ in *physical form* (liquid, gas, or solid), in *chemical form* (and therefore in their potential environmental impact), and in the *nature* of the radiation they emit (see Types of Radiation in Chapter 3). Since radiation is a form of energy and since much of the energy released is trapped and remains in the waste material itself, radioactive waste generates heat; how hot a particular kind of waste is influences the manner of its disposal.

The federal government has defined radioactive waste forms as follows:

Spent fuel consists of irradiated fuel removed from a commercial reactor (after three or four years in use) or special fuels from test or research reactors. Spent fuel is highly radioactive and generates a lot of heat; it requires heavy shielding (that is, a material, such as concrete, water, or lead, placed between a radiation source and a person for protection against the danger of radiation) and remote handling (that is, no human contact). After spent fuel assemblies are removed from a reactor, they are submerged in water in large pools to be cooled and to protect people from their radioactivity. Most commercial spent fuel is stored in on-site pools at nuclear power plants. Since there are no present plans to reprocess commercial spent fuel (see Reprocessing, p. 14), and since the assemblies contain unused uranium, fission products and transuranic elements, including plutonium—they are considered a form of high-level waste. Special government-owned spent fuel that is not routinely reprocessed is stored at federal facilities in Idaho and South Carolina.

High-level waste (HLW) is generated by the reprocessing (that is, the chemical separation of the uranium and plutonium from the fission products and transuranic elements in the spent fuel) of either commercial spent fuel or defense production reactor fuel. High-level waste is liquid unless it has been chemically treated, in which case it may be a mixture of liquid and sludge or calcine, a dry granular material. High-level waste generates a lot of heat and requires heavy shielding to control penetrating radiation. It must be handled remotely.

Transuranic waste (TRU) comes primarily from the reprocessing of spent fuel and from the use of plutonium in the fabrication of nuclear weapons. It is defined by the Department of Energy as "waste contaminated with alpha-emitting radionuclides of atomic number greater than 92 (that is, uranium; hence the term transuranic) and half-lives greater than 20 years in concentrations greater than 100 nanocuries per gram." Transuranic waste is less intensely radioactive and generates less heat than fission products, but it normally takes a long time to decay and thus requires the same sort of long-term isolation as high-level waste. Generally, little or no shielding is required, but some TRU waste does require shielding or remote handling.

Low-level waste (LLW) includes all radioactive waste not classified as uranium mill tailings, transuranic waste, high-level waste, spent nuclear fuel, or byproduct material. While most low-level wastes are relatively short-lived and have low radioactivity, some may present a significant radiation hazard. Low-level wastes are generated by institutions and facilities using radioactive materials—hospitals, laboratories, industrial plants, nuclear power plants, government and defense laboratories and reactors. It comes in a variety of forms—animal carcasses, medical treatment and research materials, contaminated wiping rags and paper towels, protective clothing, hand tools, obsolete equipment, and so forth. The radiation from low-level waste sometimes is high enough to require shielding for handling and shipment. The Nuclear Regulatory Commission has developed a classification system for low-level waste based on its potential hazards and has specified the type of packaging as well as the form of burial required for each of the three general classes of waste—A, B, and C.

Uranium Mill Tailings are the earthen residues, usually in the form of fine sand, that remain after mining and the extraction of uranium from ores. Tailings are produced in very large volumes and contain low concentrations of naturally occurring radioactive materials, including thorium-230 and radium-226, which decays to emit the radioactive gas radon-222.

Naturally occurring and accelerator-produced radioactive material (NARM) is another category of waste. Examples of naturally occurring wastes are radium-226, which is found in smoke detectors and watch dials, and polonium-210, which is found in industrial gauges. An example of an accelerator-produced radioactive material is cobalt-57, which is produced in linear accelerators for making medical instruments. The NRC does not have the authority under the Atomic Energy Act to regulate this type of waste.

Figure 2 summarizes the existing quantities of each waste type.

Figure 2: Current and Projected Quantities of Radioactive Waste and Spent Fuel (September 1983)

Types of Waste	Volume of waste (measurements in thousand cubic meters)		
	1983	2000	2010
High-level waste (HLW)			
Commercial	2.3	.436	3.17
Defense	304	294	269
Transuranic waste (TRU)			
Commercial	—	4.6	49.4
Defense	246	340	397
Spent Fuel[1]			
Commercial	4.626	19.378	33.258
Defense	0	0	0
Low-level waste (LLW)			
Commercial	1,020	3,393	5,415
Defense	2,060	3,720	4,710
Inactive uranium mill tailings[2]	14,314	23,700	23,700
Active mill tailings[3]	96,500	188,800	280,300

(DOE/Defense tailings are about 35% of these totals.)

Source: Adapted from *Spent Fuel and Radioactive Waste Inventories, Projections and Characteristics.* U.S. Department of Energy, September 1984.

1. No reprocessing.
2. Found primarily at inactive uranium mills located in western United States. DOE responsible for stabilization and control of mill tailings in safe and environmentally sound manner under the Uranium Mill Tailings Radiation Control Act of 1978. Anticipated cleanup completion in late 1980s.
3. Located at the 16 active licensed uranium mills operating in 1983, all in the western United States.

NUCLEAR FUEL CYCLE

Although there are many sources of nuclear waste, for a number of reasons much of the controversy today stems from disputes over what to do with wastes from commercial nuclear power plants. One reason is that regulation of commercial plants is subject to citizen review. In addition, these plants are big and, unlike many defense operations, highly visible; they also generate large quantities of radioactive waste. And, of course, some citizens categorically oppose the use of nuclear power to generate electricity.

But nuclear power plant operation is only one stage in the commercial nuclear fuel cycle. Each stage of the cycle produces radioactive wastes:

Uranium mining   Routine ventilation of mines results in the release of radon gas and uranium-bearing dust.

Milling   Uranium ore is crushed, ground, and chemically processed to produce a compound (U_3O_8) known as "yellowcake." This operation releases small amounts of radon gas and uranium dust. After the refining process, the tailings are pumped in slurry form to a settling pond. The water gradually dissipates through seepage and evaporation, eventually leaving behind huge piles of relatively dry, finely ground tailings that contain radium (which decays into radon) and other long-lived radioisotopes, especially thorium-230.

Conversion   Yellowcake is converted to uranium hexafluoride (UF_6). Depending on the technique used, the process produces wastes that are either mostly solid or a sludge, with a small part discharged as gas. These wastes contain mainly radium and some uranium and thorium.

Enrichment   With the application of heat, UF_6 becomes a gas that permits the concentration (enrichment) of uranium-235, the uranium isotope required for reactor fuel. In this process, small quantities of radioactive gas are vented directly into the atmosphere and some liquid waste from cleanup operations is diluted and discharged to the environment.

Fuel fabrication   Enriched UF_6 gas is converted chemically to solid uranium dioxide (UO_2), which is formed into ceramic pellets that are placed in zircalloy cladding to make fuel rods. These are bundled together into fuel assemblies containing fifty to three hundred rods. The radioactive wastes resulting from these operations include gases and liquid waste containing very small quantities of uranium and thorium.

Power plant operation   As the uranium-235 fuel in the nuclear reactor fissions and generates heat for electric power production, the fission fragments (products) accumulate and gradually reduce the efficiency of the chain reaction. After an average use of three

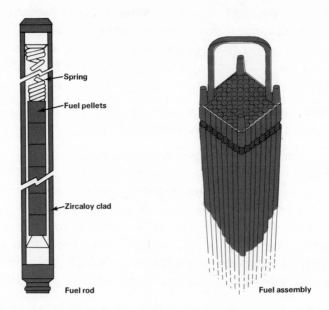

Spring

Fuel pellets

Zircaloy clad

Fuel rod   Fuel assembly

Figure 3. Fuel rod and fuel assembly. Even during the high temperature and pressure of reactor operation, essentially all waste products remain locked in the dense uranium pellet and the zirconium metal cladding making up the fuel assemblies. *"Closing the Circle," Atomic Industrial Forum*

to four years, spent fuel rods are then removed from the reactor. As noted above, currently almost all spent fuel rods are being stored underwater in large pools at reactor sites. Other radioactive wastes generated at nuclear power plants include fission product gases such as krypton and xenon; filter media left over from treating contaminated cooling and cleaning water; and miscellaneous solid wastes, such as protective clothing and cleaning paper.

Reprocessing   During this stage unconsumed uranium and plutonium are chemically separated from the fission products in the spent fuel so they can be used again. But, as noted earlier, commercial spent fuel is not being reprocessed in the United States at the present time. (See Reprocessing, page 14)

DECOMMISSIONING

Outmoded or inoperable nuclear power plants and plant equipment constitute another potentially large source of nuclear wastes. Generally, a reactor's economically useful lifetime is predicted to be from thirty to forty years. During the fission process, neutrons bombard not only the uranium fuel but other parts of a nuclear reactor as well. Some strike the steel structures that support the fuel or the steel reactor vessel that holds both the fuel rods and the coolant, and some even make their way into the massive concrete containment structure that shields the reactor vessel. During the life of the reactor some neutrons are absorbed by atoms of cobalt, iron, nickel, and other elements in the steel, water, and concrete.

Because some of the resulting isotopes, called activation products, will remain highly radioactive for several decades or more, a nuclear power plant must be closed down, or "decommissioned," in a way that will prevent public exposure to or dispersion of radioactivity. While a number of small experimental reactors have been decommissioned so far in the United States, only one small commercial reactor, the Elk River Plant in Minnesota (58 megawatts), has been fully dismantled (1974). A second and larger (72 MW) commercial nuclear power plant at Shippingport, Pennsylvania, is scheduled to be dismantled over the next few years. Shippingport operated from 1957 until 1982 as a government demonstration and test facility, selling power to the Duquesne Light Company. The plant is again being used as a demonstration, this time in decommissioning. The Department of Energy's $98 million decommissioning plan calls for dismantling the plant and shipping its radioactive parts to the Hanford Reservation near Richland, Washington, for burial. The rest of the Shippingport plant structure will be demolished. The total process should be completed by 1990.

There are three approaches to decommissioning that are recognized worldwide:

Immediate dismantlement. This method entails decontamination of the power plant and removal of all radioactive components (solid and liquid) to a radioactive waste-disposal facility. Upon completion, the nuclear license is terminated and the property is released for unrestricted use. The Elk River Plant is the first commercial light-water reactor to be fully dismantled. The Shippingport plant will be the second.

Safe storage, with later dismantlement. Under this approach, most of the radioactive materials are removed, and contaminated areas are decontaminated or secured. The plant is then isolated to allow for further radioactive decay. The structures and equipment to be dismantled later are securely maintained to protect the public from residual radioactivity. Once the plant is completely dismantled, the property will be released for unrestricted use. A number of research and demonstration reactors are now in safe storage.

Entombment. This method consists of sealing the reactor with concrete or steel, after liquid waste, fuel, and surface contamination have been removed to the greatest extent possible. The structure remains entombed for a period of time sufficient to permit the decay of radioactivity to unrestricted release levels. The property must be guarded to protect against intrusion. Three small research or experimental reactors—in Hullam, Nebraska, Piqua, Ohio, and Ricon, Puerto Rico—have been entombed.

In sum, the front end of the fuel cycle—uranium mining and milling—presently generates the largest quantity of radioactive waste, in the form of uranium tailings; the back end of the cycle—reprocessing or intact spent fuel assemblies from nuclear power plants—produces virtually all the high-level and transuranic wastes.

Reprocessing and the Nuclear Fuel Cycle

The commercial nuclear power system that exists today in the United States is dominated by one kind of reactor, the light-water reactor (LWR), and by a fuel cycle based on once-through uranium use. ("Once-through" means that only fresh uranium oxide fuel is used; spent fuel, rather than being reprocessed, is being stored until a method of permanent disposal is established.) In contrast, spent fuel from defense reactors is always reprocessed, since the primary purpose of defense reactors is the production of uranium and plutonium for use in nuclear weapons.

Originally, the light-water reactor was designed with the reprocessing and reuse of the usable uranium and plutonium in spent nuclear fuel in mind. Reprocessing of some commercial spent fuel did take place in the early 1970s but soon ceased because regulatory and technical problems made the operation uneconomic. But there are larger issues involved as well. The once-through cycle employs uranium fuel in a form that cannot be used for nuclear weapons. The reprocessing of spent fuel separates out both unused U-235 and plutonium, the stuff of which nuclear weapons are made. The fissioning of the uranium fuel in light-water reactors creates plutonium that in turn fissions and helps generate energy. If this plutonium is never separated from the fuel by reprocessing, it never appears in a form accessible for nuclear weapons. For that reason both President Ford and President Carter imposed indefinite bans on commercial reprocessing, although other nations did not follow the U.S. initiative.

In 1981, President Reagan lifted the U.S. moratorium on reprocessing of commercial spent fuel. But although there is no longer a government ban, private industry has no plans at the present time to pursue reprocessing because of unfavorable economics and uncertainty about future government policies. Reprocessing of spent fuel for weapons production by the federal government continues.

3

Radiation Hazards

▼　　　▼　　　▼　　　▼　　　▼

Nuclear wastes are hazardous because they are radioactive; they emit either nuclear particles (alpha or beta particles) or pure energy radiation in the form of gamma rays, which are similar to X rays. (See below for more on types of radiation.) Because these radioactive particles or rays are energetic, they can cause damage. As they travel through human tissue, for example, they rip electrons from the molecules and atoms they strike or pass near, leaving the molecule or atom "ionized," that is, charged electrically. These ionized particles and the ejected electrons can cause death or damage to cells and cell components.

The nature and severity of the damage depend on what is struck, on the amount of radiation—the exposure—that strikes the body or specific organs or tissues, and on the sensitivity of the struck cell. The basic requirement, therefore, of a nuclear waste management program is to prevent this potential damage by isolating the radioactive wastes to limit or prevent their release into the environment until they have decayed to low levels or stable forms that pose little threat to human health.

SOURCES OF RADIATION

Natural radioactive isotopes in the earth (primarily uranium, thorium, radium, and potassium) and cosmic rays, filtered through the atmosphere from outer space, immerse us in a constant flux of

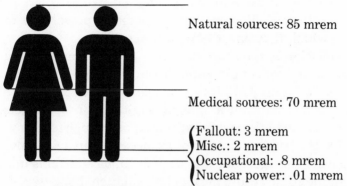

Natural sources: 85 mrem

Medical sources: 70 mrem

{ Fallout: 3 mrem
  Misc.: 2 mrem
  Occupational: .8 mrem
  Nuclear power: .01 mrem

Total: 160.81 mrem (average dose for U.S. citizen)

Figure 4. Estimated annual whole body radiation dose in the United States. From "*Nuclear Power: Issues and Choices and Energy in Transition: 1985–2010.*"

radiation. In addition to this natural background radiation, people are exposed to several man-made sources of radiation: medical applications, such as X rays; fallout from past nuclear weapons testing; and consumer goods, such as color television sets. Of the approximately one hundred sixty millirems of radiation to which the "average" person living in the United States is exposed every year, 50 percent comes from natural sources and 50 percent from human activities. Medical diagnosis and therapy account for more than 90 percent of the man-made dose (see Figure 4).

Some activities, occupations, and areas expose a person to a greater-than-average radiation dose. For example, a person living at an altitude of five thousand feet in Denver, Colorado, receives nearly twice as much cosmic radiation from outer space as a person living at sea level in Washington, D.C. Similarly, high concentrations of radioactive minerals in beach sands in Brazil and India expose the local residents to as much as ten times the normal levels of natural radiation.

TYPES OF RADIATION

The radioactive isotopes found in nature, commercial products, and nuclear wastes emit three forms of radiation. While all are potentially harmful, they differ in their penetrating power and in the manner in which they affect human tissue.

Alpha radiation is the most energetic (densely ionizing) but the least penetrating type of radiation. It can be stopped by a sheet of paper. Although alpha particles are unable to penetrate human skin, they may be very harmful if an alpha-emitting isotope enters the body through a cut or through breathing air or through food or water. Once inside the body, the radioisotope decays, causing highly concentrated local damage. For example, if an alpha emitter is inhaled, the lung tissue could absorb most of the radiation. Long-lived transuranics such as plutonium are alpha emitters.

Beta radiation is a more penetrating type of ionizing radiation. Some beta particles can penetrate skin but, like alpha particles, beta-emitting isotopes may cause the most serious effects when they are inhaled or ingested. Most fission products in spent-fuel assemblies and reprocessed waste (e.g., iodine-131, cesium-137, and strontium-90) are beta emitters. The chemical similarities of some of these radioisotopes to naturally occurring elements in the body lead them to seek certain organs in the body. For example, the chemical resemblance of strontium-90 to calcium results in its concentration in the bones, where it may remain and cause continued exposure.

Gamma radiation (high-energy electromagnetic energy waves) has the greatest penetrating power and usually accompanies beta emission. Gamma rays are similar to X rays (they are both electromagnetic radiation) but they have different penetrating power. Gamma radiation can penetrate and damage critical organs in the body. Most fission products are gamma emitters as well as beta emitters.

In high-level waste, beta and gamma radiation dominate for the first five hundred to one thousand years; after that, alpha-emitting isotopes in the wastes present the greatest hazard. Since some alpha emitters have very long half-lives, some may remain radioactive for as long as millions of years (see "Hazardous For How Long?" below). Transuranic waste, TRU-contaminated objects, and uranium mill tailings are major sources of alpha radiation. Low-level wastes emit alpha, beta, and gamma radiation.

MEASURES OF RADIATION

The damage to living material from radiation depends on the energy that is transmitted to the cell and its constituents and on the number of cells struck. These in turn depend on the type of radiation and on the dose—that is, on the total amount of radiation energy absorbed by the struck tissue.

What is needed, therefore, in order to compare the possible biological effects of radiation on humans is some measure that takes into account the amount of energy deposited (in a gram of material, for instance) and the way in which it is deposited. The way scientists reach such measurements can sound very technical and daunting to the lay person, but it is important that citizens understand the basic concepts.

The *amount*—the radiation dose—is measured in either rads or rems (see below). The *biological effect*, however, is quite different if the radiation is in the form of X rays, for instance, which only strike a molecule here and there along their path, or in the form of alpha particles, which have short paths with intense damage.

Both of these variables are roughly taken into account in the measurement called the rem (roentgen equivalent man). It represents the radiation dose that is equivalent in biological damage to 1 rad of 250-kilowatt X rays.

The rem is obtained by multiplying the dosage of a certain radiation (measured in roentgens) by a number, the RBE (for relative biological effectiveness), which takes into account the difference in the biological damage. For X rays the RBE is 1. It is 1 for moderately energetic beta particles, 1.7 or 2 for low-energy betas and 20 for alpha particles. These are obviously rough measures, and the full range of differences is even more subtle.

With this background, the various measurements are summarized below:

Rad (radiation absorbed dose) measures the amount, or dose, of ionizing radiation absorbed by any material, such as human tissue. A millirad (mrad) is a thousandth of a rad.

Roentgen measures the amount of energy lost in air by the passage of gamma or X rays.

Rem (roentgen equivalent man) is a quantity used in radiation protection to measure the amount of damage to human tissue from

Figure 5. Annual dose rates from each of the important sources of radiation exposure in the United States. *The Effects on Populations of Exposure to Low Levels of Ionizing Radiation: 1980* (National Research Council)

Source	Exposed Group			Average Dose Rate, mrems/yr	
	Description	No. Exposed	Body Portion Exposed	Exposed Group	Prorated over Total Population
Natural background					
Cosmic radiation	Total population	220×10^6	Whole body	28	28
Terrestrial radiation	Total population	220×10^6	Whole body	26	26
Internal Sources	Total population	220×10^6	Gonads	28	28
			Bone marrow	24	24
Medical x rays					
Medical diagnosis	Adult patients	105×10^6/yr	Bone marrow	103	77
Medical personnel	Occupational	195,000	Whole body	300–350[a]	0.3
Dental diagnosis	Adult patients	105×10^6/yr	Bone marrow	3	1.4
Dental personnel	Occupational	171,000	Whole body	50–125[a]	0.05
Radiopharmaceuticals					
Medical diagnosis	Patients	10×10^6 to 12×10^6/yr	Bone marrow	300	13.6
Medical personnel	Occupational	100,000	Whole body	260–350	0.1
Atmospheric weapons tests	Total population	220×10^6	Whole body	4–5	4–5
Nuclear industry					
Commercial nuclear power plants (effluent releases)	Population within 10 mi	$<10 \times 10^6$	Whole body	<<10	<<1
Commercial nuclear power plants (occupational)	Workers	67,000	Whole body	400[b]	0.1
Industrial radiography (occupational)	Workers	11,250	Whole body	320	0.02
Fuel processing and fabrication	Workers	11,250	Whole body	160	0.01

Source	Population	Number	Body part	Average dose (mrems/yr)	Genetically significant dose
Handling byproduct materials (occupational)	Workers	3,500	Whole body	350	0.01
Federal contractors (occupational)	Workers	88,500	Whole body	~250	0.1
Naval nuclear propulsion program (occupational)	Workers	36,000	Whole body	220	0.04
Research activities					
Particle accelerators (occupational)	Workers	10,000	Whole body	Unknown	<<1
X-ray diffraction units (occupational)	Workers	10,000–20,000	Extremities and whole body	Unknown	<<1
Electron microscopes (occupational)	Workers	4,400	Whole body	50–200	0.003
Neutron generators (occupational)	Workers	1,000–2,000	Whole body	Unknown	<<1
Consumer products					
Building materials	Population in brick and masonry buildings	100×10^6	Whole body	7	3–4
Television receivers	Viewing populations		Gonads	0.2–1.5	0.5
Miscellaneous					
Airline travel (cosmic radiation)	Passengers	35×10^{6c}	Whole body	3	0.5
	Crew members and flight attendants	40,000	Whole body	160	0.03
Airline transport of radioactive materials	Passengers	7×10^{6d}	Whole body	~0.3	0.01
	Crew members and flight attendants	40,000	Whole body	~3	<0.001

[a] Based on personnel dosimeter readings; because of relatively low energy of medical x rays, actual whole-body doses are probably less.

[b] Average dose rate to the approximately 40,000 workers who received measurable exposures was 600–800 mrems/yr.

[c] Total number of revenue passengers per year is 210×10^6; however, many of these are repeat airline travelers.

[d] About one in every 30 airline flights includes the transportation of radioactive materials; assuming 210×10^6 passengers per year (total), approximately 7×10^6 would be on flights carrying radioactive materials.

a dose of ionizing radiation. It takes into account both the *amount* of radiation deposited in body tissues and the *type* of radiation— alpha, beta, or gamma radiation. A millirem is a thousandth of a rem.

Man-rem (also person-rem) measures the total radiation dose received by a population. It is the average radiation dose in rems multiplied by the number of people in the population group.

BIOLOGICAL EFFECTS

Radiation can kill or damage cells. If enough cells die, the organ they form will die; if crucial organs die, the organism will die. Thus, one consequence of radiation is death.

To be immediately lethal, radiation exposure to the whole body must exceed one thousand rems over a brief period—minutes or hours (such exposures occurred at the Hiroshima and Nagasaki bombings). A dose of four hundred rems, delivered at one time to the whole body, will cause death, on the average, in 50 percent of the cases.

In the range from four hundred rems down to one hundred rems, radiation sickness occurs and some individuals will die. At lower radiation levels, the consequences are more difficult to predict and detect.

For low radiation doses it is cell damage, not cell death, that is harmful. A few dead cells can be replaced or repaired. Damage, however, can replicate itself and multiply. The type of damage resulting from radiation depends on the nature of the struck cell.

If it is an "ordinary" cell—bone or organ tissue, for instance— the damage is confined to the struck organism. This is called *somatic* damage. The most feared type of somatic damage is cancer. However, damage to a reproductive cell can cause genetic damage through a *mutation*, transmitting the damage to future generations.

That radiation can cause cancer or genetic mutation is not in doubt. What is questioned is the relationship between the dose— particularly doses below one rem—and the incidence of resulting cancers or mutations. For both types of damage, the latency period— the time between exposure and the effect—is long. It can be twenty-five or so years for cancer and a generation or more for genetic damage. And in both cases, other possible causes—chemical car-

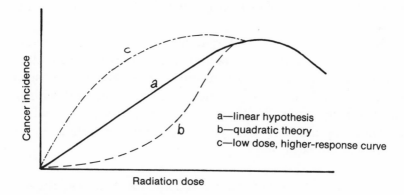

Figure 6. Dose response curves. The curves eventually level off and then decrease at high doses of radiation since more cells die than become cancerous. Source: *Report of the Interagency Task Force on the Health Effects of Ionizing Radiation, June 1979*, U.S. Department of Health, Education and Welfare

cinogens, for example—can confuse the issue and make it difficult or impossible to trace the origin of the damage.

Despite uncertainties and difficulties, however, scientists have developed several mathematical methods to predict the effects of low-level radiation. One is the *linear hypothesis*, which is based on two assumptions: first, that there is *no* threshold level below which radiation has no carcinogenic (cancer-causing) effect; and second, that the incidence of cancer at low doses is directly proportional to the incidence at high-dose levels. Using this hypothesis, the known dose-response for high levels of radiation is plotted on a graph and the dose-response for low levels is extrapolated by drawing a straight line from the known data to zero (see line *a* in Figure 6).

Many scientists, including most of those who served on the 1980 Advisory Committee on the Biological Effects of Ionizing Radiations (BEIR III) of the National Academy of Sciences,[1] believe that the linear hypothesis overestimates the risks of low-level radiation. They subscribe to the *linear quadratic theory*, which predicts that cancer incidence is proportionately lower at low doses than at high doses, in part because body cells may repair themselves more easily at low doses (see line *b* in Figure 6).

A third possible alternative, one that few in the scientific community accept, suggests that the linear hypothesis may *under-*

estimate the risk of cancer from low-level radiation (see line *c* in Figure 6).

One reason for these different theories is that, in general, risk estimates for low levels of radiation are based on sparse data and involve a large degree of uncertainty. Philip Handler, president of the National Academy of Sciences, discussed this uncertainty and the resulting scientific disagreement in his July 22, 1980, letter transmitting the BEIR III report to the Environmental Protection Agency administrator.

> Generally, the sparser and less reliable the data base, the more opportunity for disagreement. In this case, there are sufficient data concerning the effects of exposure to high doses of ionizing radiation, but little reliable information concerning the consequences of exposure to lower doses, especially those low doses to which a human population might be exposed. Upon the issue of how one may extrapolate from the high doses to the low, scientific argument turned on the question of how one may validly extrapolate from the measured effects of high doses to the most probable effects of low doses.[2]

Federal agencies use the linear hypothesis as the theoretical basis for setting current radiation exposure standards. In the absence of firm data, they feel it provides maximum assurance that public health will be protected.

The Environmental Protection Agency (EPA) is the federal agency charged with establishing standards limiting the radiation dose to the general population from nuclear power plants and also from other parts of the nuclear fuel cycle. These standards have been continually revised to make them more stringent since the federal government began setting radiation limits in 1957. Currently, the EPA limit for the general population is set at a 25-mrem whole-body dose from nuclear facilities such as fuel fabrication plants or power plants each year. The agency does not claim that this is a risk-free level, but rather, a level at which the risk of health effects is balanced against the benefits of nuclear power. It is generally thought that this "risk" is well within the range of risks accepted for other methods of generating electricity.

THE URANIUM—238 DECAY CHAIN*

Radiation Emitted			Radioactive Elements	Half-life		
Alpha	Beta	Gamma		Minutes	Days	Years
☢		☢	Uranium-238			4.5 BILL
	☢	☢	Thorium-234		24.1	
	☢	☢	Protactinium-234	1.2		
☢		☢	Uranium-234			247,000
☢		☢	Thorium-230			80,000
☢		☢	Radium-226			1,622
☢			Radon-222		3.8	
☢	☢		Polonium-218	3.0		
	☢	☢	Lead-214	26.8		
☢	☢	☢	Bismuth-214	19.7		
☢			Polonium-214	(0.00016 second)		
	☢	☢	Lead-210			22
☢	☢		Bismuth-210		5.0	
☢		☢	Polonium-210		138.3	
NONE			Lead-206			STABLE

*Simplified; data from Lipschutz 1980.
Three other decay chains exist.

Figure 7. The Uranium-238 Decay Chain
Source: *Radioactive Waste: Issues and Answers,*
American Institute of Professional Geologists

HAZARDOUS FOR HOW LONG?

How long will nuclear wastes remain hazardous? Some experts propose that an isolation time of three hundred to five hundred years for high-level waste is adequate, and others refer to the "million year" waste-disposal problem. There are several reasons for the wide discrepancy in estimates. One is the wide latitude available to participants in the nuclear debate in choosing a level of acceptable risk for a given benefit.

Another is the vast difference in half-lives among the different radioisotopes in wastes. Each radioisotope has its own half-life, which is the time it takes to lose 50 percent of its activity by decay. The activity or rate of decay decreases with time in the same way that the number of atoms present decreases. Thus the hazard due to radioactive emissions decreases with time. The important fission products (strontium-90 and cesium-137) have half-lives of about thirty years, in contrast with twenty-four thousand years for the much less abundant plutonium.

Experts who talk of isolating high-level waste for three hundred to five hundred years base this figure on the average half-life of cesium and strontium and assume that after about ten half-lives (10 × 30-year average half-life = 300 years), the radioactivity level of the high-level waste will be low enough (about a thousandth of the original) not to pose a significant hazard. Others, who propose isolating wastes up to a million years, base their estimate on the longer-lived radioisotopes such as the transuranic element plutonium. They believe that these radioisotopes, though present in much smaller quantities than are fission products, still pose a significant hazard.

Most low-level waste will decay to the hazard level of uranium ore after one hundred years, according to Department of Energy officials. This is because most of the radioisotopes in low-level waste are shorter-lived than those found in high-level waste.

4

Waste Management —Past and Present

▼　　▼　　▼　　▼　　▼

Only in recent years has the federal government initiated major efforts to plan for the permanent disposal of nuclear wastes. Pushed by public insistence and a greater appreciation by scientists and policymakers of the importance of the problems, Congress has now provided a framework for solving the problems in two major pieces of legislation: the Low-Level Radioactive Waste Policy Act of 1980 and the Nuclear Waste Policy Act of 1982 (both are discussed in Chapter 5). To understand the programs laid out in the legislation and the public climate in which progress toward solutions is being pursued, it is important first to review past approaches to solving the two distinct problems of high-level and low-level nuclear wastes.

HIGH-LEVEL WASTES FROM REPROCESSING

The atomic weapons program generated the first high-level waste in the early 1940s. Fuel rods irradiated in reactors were processed to recover the uranium, plutonium, and tritium needed for weapons production. The resulting liquid high-level radioactive waste was stored in large, single-wall carbon steel underground tanks built for the purpose at the U.S. Hanford Reservation at Richland, Washington. It was assumed that permanent disposal could take place later.

The waste was acidic, and, to impede corrosion of the tanks, it was neutralized with sodium hydroxide before being pumped into them. Unfortunately, this solution to one problem led to another problem because neutralization increased the waste volume and created a sludgelike sediment in the tanks that has complicated subsequent efforts to exhume and solidify the waste.

In the early 1950s, double-wall rather than single-wall tanks were built for storage of defense-related high-level waste at the Idaho National Engineering Laboratory in Idaho and the Savannah River Plant in South Carolina. At Savannah River, where the tanks were constructed of carbon steel, the acidic high-level waste was neutralized. At Idaho Falls, where the tanks were stainless steel, the waste was initially stored untreated.

In 1956 the first tank leak at the Hanford reservation was detected. Since that time, some 450,000 gallons of high-level waste have leaked from 20 of the 149 tanks in service there. The surrounding soil has absorbed the wastes, and to date no serious groundwater pollution has been reported from these leaks. In 1960 one of the Savannah River tanks leaked about 100 gallons of high-level waste and contaminated some nearby groundwater.

In the 1960s the Atomic Energy Commission began the process of solidifying the stored high-level wastes to stabilize them and reduce the volume. The neutralized wastes at Hanford and Savannah River were evaporated, leaving a reduced mixture of liquid, sludge, and salt cake in the carbon steel tanks. At the Idaho Falls facility, where the high-level wastes had not been neutralized, they were converted into calcine, a dry granular material that is stored in stainless steel bins that are then encased in underground concrete vaults.

When the first commercial reprocessing plant was built in West Valley, New York, in the 1960s, the Atomic Energy Commission approved the same waste-storage system—carbon steel tanks and neutralized wastes—used at Hanford. However, to deal with the problems identified at Hanford, the individual tanks were placed in saucers to catch any leakage and installed in underground concrete vaults. During its six years of operation, the West Valley plant produced and stored about 600,000 gallons of high-level waste from the reprocessing of commercial spent fuel and some spent fuel from the Hanford defense reactor.

In the late 1970s the federal government began to give serious attention to more effectively isolating from the environment wastes generated by weapons production. Twenty new tanks with improved leak-detection devices were built at Hanford and twenty-seven at Savannah River. The original intent was to eliminate the single-wall steel tanks, but a serious catch was discovered. While the liquid high-level waste could be pumped from the old tanks to the new ones, the nitric acid process required to redissolve the neutralized sludge and the solidified salt cake also corroded the walls of the old tank. Furthermore, steelwork protruding into the sludge from the floor of the tanks at Savannah River interfered with attempts to remove the sediment mechanically.

Several major research projects are currently under way at Savannah River, Hanford, and West Valley to resolve these problems. Research at Savannah River has demonstrated a successful method of removing the sludge and liquid high-level waste from the steel tanks located there, and a new facility is now under construction to convert the waste into glass. Plans being developed at Hanford call for wastes from the single-wall tanks to be partitioned, with the highly radioactive portion solidified for later disposal in a geologic repository and the low-activity portion disposed of on-site immobilized in grout. Other, difficult-to-move wastes may be stabilized in place. Under a joint federal/state project, the West Valley reprocessing plant is being decontaminated and a ceramic melter installed to demonstrate a method of solidifying the high-level radioactive waste and to process the on-site waste into a glass form.

Critics consider the government's track record for managing high-level waste to be dismal. But federal officials argue that if one considers the amount of waste stored, the fraction that has leaked is very small—less than one percent. They point to current major efforts to correct the problems and emphasize that most of the leakage has occurred at Hanford, Washington, where tanks were not so carefully constructed because of wartime pressures and supply problems (e.g., stainless steel was not readily available). Nuclear industry representatives emphasize that past mistakes in managing high-level waste have involved mostly defense, not commercial, wastes.

SPENT FUEL

Storage facilities for spent fuel rods originally were designed on the assumption that spent fuel would be stored under water for about five months at reactor sites and then shipped away for reprocessing and final disposal of the remaining waste. Such a system, based on reprocessing, has not materialized (see Reprocessing, on page 14), and utilities have faced numerous changes in federal policy and regulations with consequent delays in the timetable for removing spent fuel from plant sites.

About 515 tons—6 percent of all spent fuel rods from commercial sources—were shipped and "temporarily" stored in deepwater pools at West Valley, New York, and Morris, Illinois, two sites originally intended as reprocessing plants for commercial spent fuel. The West Valley facility did reprocess some commercial spent fuel rods before it closed in 1972, but the Morris plant never operated because of design problems.

The spent fuel that was stored at the West Valley facility awaiting reprocessing is now being returned to the nuclear power plants from which it originated. In contrast, the Morris site is still being used for spent fuel storage, and it continues to accept spent fuel from three utilities under existing contracts. However, the storage capacity of the Morris facility—approximately 720 metric tons—is fully committed under those contracts.

Thus, most spent fuel rods are being stored in pools on reactor sites around the country, and some of these pools are filling up rapidly. To deal with this problem, utilities are increasing their storage capacity (a step that must be licensed by the Nuclear Regulatory Commission) by reracking fuel-assembly storage modules in existing pools, by expanding on-site storage capability, and by transshipping, or moving the spent fuel to another reactor site. With the support and encouragement of the Department of Energy, utilities also are investigating alternative storage options, including a system that would use the same cask for dry storage of spent fuel at a reactor site and for transportation to the federal storage or disposal facility when it becomes available. Methods for consolidating fuel racks also are being tested. According to a January 1983 Department of Energy report,[3] even if utilities are able to rerack their pools and transship to the maximum extent practical, storage will be a problem at some reactors beginning in the late 1980s unless

Figure 8. At-reactor storage of spent fuel. Some sixty assemblies of used fuel are discharged about once a year by a typical large power reactor. Highly radioactive, these spent fuel assemblies are stored under water in steel-lined concrete pools, mostly at plant sites. Source: *"Closing the Circle"*, Atomic Industrial Forum

new technologies are developed, licensed, and available for utility use before that time.

A number of states and localities have raised concerns about increased storage of spent fuel at reactor sites. Some oppose reracking because they fear that increasing the density of fuel rods in a pool might trigger a chain reaction. This fear seems unwarranted, because for such a reaction to occur, the rods would not only have to be packed with very precise spacing but the water moderating the reaction also would have to be free of the chemical inhibitor used in the storage pools. The water circulating through the pools acts as a coolant and neutron absorber, and even though some fissioning continues to occur, the fuel steadily decreases in temperature. Other localities oppose additional on-site storage by any method, fearing that power plant sites might become de facto long-term storage or disposal sites if federal facilities fail to materialize as scheduled.

Under provisions of the Nuclear Waste Policy Act of 1982 (see Chapter 5), the Department of Energy is responsible for ensuring that power plants are not forced to shut down for lack of spent-fuel storage capacity. In addition to helping utilities develop additional storage capacity, the agency is charged with developing contingency plans for last-resort federal interim storage. The act specifies that this storage capacity is to be limited to not more than nineteen hundred metric tons of spent fuel. The Department of Energy stated in its 1983 draft mission plan that it does not anticipate that any federal storage will be required. However, the question of whether and how much federal interim storage is needed ultimately will be determined in large part by the ability of the nuclear power industry to develop its own additional storage capacity.

At one time it was thought that the United States nonproliferation policy might add to the need for storage capacity in this country. As part of that policy, agreements for the sale of United States technology or nuclear supplies to a foreign country contain the provision that the United States must approve the disposition of spent fuel from the resulting reactors. The original assumption was that the spent fuel would be shipped back to this country for storage. Recently, however, the United States has granted approval to several countries to reprocess the fuel rather than return it to this country. Only a small amount of spent fuel from foreign research and test reactors is now being returned to the United States for storage at Idaho Falls, Idaho, and Savannah River, South Carolina.

In sum, while the Department of Energy has contracted with utilities to begin to accept their spent fuel in 1998, some difficult questions remain. Will federal storage or disposal facilities in fact be ready by that date? Will the Department of Energy be able to accept the fuel at a rate that will prevent possible overcrowding in power-plant storage capacity? These uncertainties concern citizens who want waste disposal decisions to be made carefully, and they also trouble utility planners who need confidence in the schedule as a basis for planning their own storage systems.

LOW-LEVEL AND TRANSURANIC WASTES

In the 1940s and 1950s, low-level wastes either were buried in shallow trenches at sites owned and operated by the federal government or were packaged in steel drums and dumped at sea. The government-owned sites were developed primarily to serve defense and governmental nuclear research activities, and in the early 1960s the government decided to restrict their use for federal wastes only. The United States government stopped issuing new ocean disposal licenses in 1960, and the last disposal at sea occurred in 1970. Currently all permanent disposal of low-level radioactive waste is in shallow land-burial facilities—commercial and government-owned.

Before 1970, some materials contaminated with transuranic radionuclides, originating primarily from defense activities, were disposed of as low-level waste at federal and commercial facilities. Over the years, some of the containers of this buried waste have been breached, and the surrounding soil has been contaminated. New requirements

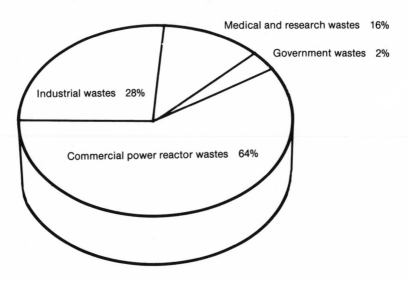

Figure 9. Volume of low-level wastes from all sources.

established by the Atomic Energy Commission in 1970 specified that transuranic waste be segregated from other radioactive waste and packaged and stored to be retrieved for later disposal in a geologic repository. The federal government has exhumed some of the transuranic waste previously buried in the federal low-level waste disposal site in Idaho and stored it there. Similar plans are under consideration for other federal sites.

Six Department of Energy sites now accept federal transuranic waste for storage. The largest inventory of transuranic waste is at Hanford; some is interred in the low-level waste burial grounds and some is stored for retrieval. Power plants must store their own small amounts of transuranic waste.

The low-level waste generated from defense and federal research facilities is disposed of at federal sites. Commercially generated low-level waste is disposed of in three commercially operated sites.

The first commercial low-level waste site was opened in 1962 at Beatty, Nevada. By 1971, six commercial sites had been established. Of those, three—West Valley, New York; Maxey Flats, Kentucky; and Sheffield, Illinois—are no longer operating. The West Valley low-level waste-disposal site, part of a larger Nuclear Fuel Services facility, was closed in 1975 because poor drainage caused the burial trenches to fill with rainwater and overflow. When state authorities in Kentucky discovered that some radioactive material had migrated from the site at Maxey Flats, they put such a high surcharge on wastes buried there that the operation soon became uneconomic and the site closed in 1977. A third site in Sheffield, Illinois, closed in 1978 when it reached its licensed capacity and could not expand because of state opposition and the denial by the Nuclear Regulatory Commission of permission to open a new trench. This leaves the low-level waste facilities at Barnwell, South Carolina, Hanford, Washington, and Beatty, Nevada, as the only operating disposal sites for commercially generated low-level wastes.

In general, water poses the most serious technical problems in shallow land burial. Water flowing over the ground may erode the cap or sides of the trench, threatening its structural integrity. Further, any water that infiltrates a trench can provide a pathway for radionuclide migration to the outside environment. A recent study found that water has come into contact with waste in burial trenches at six of the eleven major government and commercial land burial facilities—Oak Ridge, Tennessee, Maxey Flats, Kentucky, West Valley, New York, Idaho Falls, Idaho, Savannah River, South Carolina, and Los Alamos, New Mexico. The main pathways appear to have been water infiltrating through the trench backfill. Other possible routes of radionuclide escape from the trenches are uptake of water-borne radionuclides by deep-rooted plants and transport to the surface of radioactive items such as paper and clothing caused by small animals burrowing into trenches.[4]

At the time when the first commercial low-level waste disposal sites were selected, uniform regulations for site selection and operation did not exist. Some of the hydrogeologic problems, including accumulation of water in trenches, erosion, and unexpected complexity in groundwater movement, encountered at those sites can be attributed to inadequate attention to earth-science criteria in site selection and design.

Most experts agree that we have learned a great deal from past difficulties and argue that the problems, whether due to faulty construction or improper siting procedures, can be prevented in the future. They point out that there are now stringent NRC regulations in place to guide the siting, operation, and closure of a shallow land burial facility.

During the 1970s the three states with commercial sites began encountering both operational and political problems. The Barnwell, South Carolina, site, the only commercial site located in the eastern half of the country—where the majority of nuclear plants and other waste generators are located—received about 85 percent of all commercial low-level waste during the 1970s. Hence the state, feeling already overburdened, refused to accept any of the voluminous low-level waste generated by the March 1979 accident at the Three Mile Island nuclear power plant. The governors of Nevada, South Carolina, and Washington, sharply critical of packaging requirements and federal enforcement of them, demanded improved federal standards. No action was taken, and in late 1979 Nevada and Washington closed their sites temporarily because trucks were delivering damaged and leaking nuclear waste containers to them. At the same time, South Carolina's Governor Riley announced that over the next two years the state would reduce by half the amount of low-level waste it would accept annually. These actions caused alarm among those who used the sites, particularly medical and

Figure 10. Burial trench for low-level
waste in "before-and-after" views.
Above, the open trench: the floor of
the trench slopes gently to the side
and end, where monitoring systems
detect, sample, collect, and remove
any moisture that may enter the
trench. Below: the filled-in trench.
Permanent markers are used for the
burial trenches. The final use of the
site may be for recreation, open
space, or any low-intensity use that
does not disturb the burial trench.
Photo: *Chem-Nuclear Systems, Inc.
From Planning Advisory Service
Report 369, "A Planner's Guide to
Low-Level Radioactive Waste
Disposal," by Thomas P. Smith.*
American Planning Association,
1982

research facilities with limited storage capacity, and provided some of the impetus behind the passage of the Low-level Radioactive Waste Policy Act in 1980.

Although all three commercial low-level waste-disposal sites are currently operating, Nevada receives only 1 percent of the nation's commercial low-level waste because of a generally unfavorable regulatory climate that includes an expensive third-party inspection system required by the state. This places the main burden on the other two sites. The Hanford, Washington, site now receives twice the volume it did in 1979—approximately 53 percent of the total; the Barnwell, South Carolina, site now receives half of its 1978 volume—approximately 46 percent of the total commercially generated low-level waste.

The low-level waste transported to commercial burial grounds comes from a number of sources. Percentages vary considerably from year to year, but in 1983 about 64 percent of the total volume came from nuclear power plants, 16 percent from medical and research facilities, 28 percent from industry, and 2 percent from government and military operations. A wide range of industrial, research, and medical activities might be seriously impeded without adequate facilities for the safe storage and disposal of low-level waste.

URANIUM MILL TAILINGS

Of all radioactive wastes, uranium mill tailings have been the most neglected. Since tailings do not contain enough radioactive materials to fall under the legal definition of "source material," the Atomic Energy Commission, during its twenty-eight-year lifetime, insisted that it had no jurisdiction over this part of the nuclear fuel cycle (in spite of the fact that nearly all uranium mined between 1947 and 1970 was produced for the federal government).

As a result, the tailings piles were abandoned and left unprotected when a uranium mill closed. These abandoned piles, amounting to 27 million tons, are located in Arizona, Colorado, New Mexico, North Dakota, Oregon, Pennsylvania, South Dakota, Texas, Utah, Washington, and Wyoming. A 1976 study revealed that radium in these tailings piles had leached from two to nine feet into the subsoil and that wind had blown the tailings close to buildings and onto land where livestock and wildlife graze. The study predicted that some of the abandoned tailings piles might contaminate groundwater in the future. Finally, it concluded that hazards from most of these piles are negligible because, although the piles emit radon, most are located in sparsely populated areas. Exceptions include a pile originally located four miles from downtown Salt Lake City and now being moved, and others near Grand Junction, Colorado, and Durango, Colorado.

Critics fault the Atomic Energy Commission most severely for allowing tailings to be used in the manufacture of building materials or as fill. In the 1960s Grand Junction firms used tailings from a closed uranium mill to manufacture concrete, later used for local construction of buildings. For almost two decades, the thirty thousand people living in these buildings were exposed to radon levels up to seven times greater than the maximum allowed for uranium miners. Since the problem was identified, the federal government has provided $12 million to replace the foundations of homes, schools, and churches. On a smaller scale, tailings also have been used in buildings in Durango, Rifle, and Riverton, Colorado, Lowman, Idaho, Shiprock, New Mexico, and Salt Lake City, Utah. Many city streets and building foundations in Denver also contain tailings.

In 1978 Congress passed the Uranium Mill Tailings Radiation Control Act in response to increasing public concern about possible health hazards from tailings. The act made the Department of Energy responsible for 24 inactive tailings piles left from uranium mining and milling operations contracted by the Atomic Energy Commission. Under the act the federal government pays 90 percent of the cleanup costs and the state pays 10 percent. Final costs probably will be higher than the originally estimated $140 million, because it is likely that a number of piles cannot be stabilized and rendered innocuous in place (by covering them with loose earth or clay, for example) and will have to be moved and treated elsewhere.

Uranium mill tailings at active mills, now more than 170 metric tons, are the responsibility of the company licensed by the NRC to operate the site. Generally they pose fewer risks than abandoned tailings because they are monitored and managed by the mill operator.

Nevertheless, seepage of radioactive materials from these tailings has occurred. Of the twenty-eight conventional uranium mills licensed in the United States, twenty-one report some degree of groundwater contamination.[5] Under the Environmental Protection Agency standards, corrective action programs must be developed to return the groundwater to purity levels normal for the area. Mitigative action has been undertaken at sixteen sites to contain the seepage and reverse the flow of groundwater. Since the uranium industry in this country is declining (only seven of the twenty-eight licensed mills are currently operating and three plan to shut down soon) and many mills are not expected ever to resume operation, the process of decontamination, decommissioning, and stabilization is now under way at a number of them.[6]

One of the worst radioactive wastes spills in U.S. history occurred in July 1979 at a uranium mine and mill site in Church Rock, New Mexico. A muddy mixture of uranium mill tailings that was stored behind an earthen dam poured through a twenty-foot crack in the dam and gushed into a stream. One hundred tons of mill tailings escaped during the hour it took workers to seal the crack. Traces of the spill were later found as far as seventy-five miles away—across the Arizona border. New Mexico health authorities ordered the owner of the mill to recover the waste and clean up any contamination.

It is clear that unless mine and mill tailings are properly managed, water contamination from tailings could become a serious problem in the West. The 1978 Uranium Mill Tailings Act clarifies and strengthens the Nuclear Regulatory Commission's authority to insist on proper tailings management by the uranium mills that it licenses. It requires states that have chosen to license such milling operations to abide by substantive standards at least as stringent as those set by the federal government.

Uranium mill tailings contain the largest volume of radioactive waste in this country. When ore is processed to extract uranium, approximately 99 percent of the mass and 85 percent of the radioactivity of the original ore is left as tailings. One principal radionuclide in the pile, thorium-230, a precursor of radon-220, has a half-life of 77,000 years. This ensures that the radioactive emissions from the tailings piles will remain for a very long time indeed. Prudent management must take into account the large volumes and the persistent nature of the potential hazard of the tailings.

TRANSPORTING NUCLEAR WASTES

A safe, reliable system for transporting nuclear wastes is crucial to any nuclear waste management program. Although wastes have been shipped since the beginning of this country's nuclear program, most have been low-level wastes. When a permanent repository opens (and possibly a monitored retrievable storage [MRS] facility as well—see p. 55), the quantity of spent fuel in shipment will increase, and for the first time high-level wastes will be moved around the country. Aware of these facts, many state and local jurisdictions and citizens have become increasingly concerned about the safety of radioactive waste shipments. They want to have some control over *what* is shipped through their boundaries, *when* it is shipped, and *how* it is shipped and packaged. Furthermore, there are conflicts between the U.S. Department of Transportation and some state and local agencies over federal preemption of state and local routing regulations.

Two federal agencies—the Department of Transportation (DOT) and the Nuclear Regulatory Commission (NRC)—share the responsibilities to develop, regulate, and enforce safety standards to ensure safe transport of radioactive wastes. DOT, under the Hazardous Materials Transportation Act of 1975, has the authority to establish standards on "any safety aspect" of the transport of hazardous (in-

Figure 11. A truck carrying radioactive waste. Shipments of large quantities of radioactive materials must be by interstate highway, and urban centers are avoided primarily by the use of bypass or beltway. Photo: *Thomas P. Smith.* From *Planning Advisory Service Report 369, "A Planner's Guide to Low-Level Radioactive Waste Disposal,"* American Planning Association, 1982

cluding radioactive) materials "by any mode" in interstate and foreign commerce. The NRC, under the Atomic Energy Act of 1954, has authority to regulate "the receipt, possession, use and transfer of radioactive materials."

To avoid possible conflicts and overlap in their regulations, the Department of Transportation and the Nuclear Regulatory Commission have agreed on their respective responsibilities. In general, DOT has responsibility for packaging and shipping standards for certain low-level radioactive materials and for general labeling, handling, placarding, loading, and unloading requirements. It also regulates the qualifications for carrier personnel. The NRC sets standards for packaging and regulating the shipment and security of containment of certain higher concentrations of radioactive materials, including large quantities, special nuclear materials, and spent nuclear fuel shipments to and from commercial nuclear power plants.

Under the provisions of the Nuclear Waste Policy Act of 1982, all shipments of commercial high-level waste and spent fuel to federal facilities (repository, monitored retrievable storage [MRS] or research center) are the responsibility of DOE's Office of Civilian Radioactive Waste Management; these shipments must comply with Department of Transportation regulations. In addition, DOE has formally agreed to transport commercial spent fuel and high-level wastes in NRC-certified shipping casks.

Finally, DOE is required by law to enter into contracts with producers of high-level waste and spent fuel to take title to the waste when it is being shipped to a federal repository. The contracts, negotiated in 1984, include provisions that cover transportation from the reactor to the repository or to a federally owned and operated interim facility such as an MRS facility. All costs are to be borne by the users of nuclear generated electricity.

Packaging

The packaging design for transportation of nuclear waste is the primary insurance against the release of radioactive contents during shipment. DOT and NRC packaging and contaminant standards are based on (1) the degree of hazard posed by specific radionuclides to be shipped; (2) the quantity of radionuclides—greater quantities require more protective packaging; and (3) the form of the radioactive materials—most are solid, but liquid and gaseous materials are also shipped. Current DOT and NRC regulations specify four different types of packaging:

Strong tight containers, in addition to being highly durable, must have a tight seal and act as a shield to prevent exposure to handlers and drivers.

Type A packages must meet the requirements for strong, tight containers and in addition be capable of preventing spills and leaks under normal driving conditions. The bulk of low-level radioactive waste is shipped by truck in these two kinds of packages.

Type B packages are designed for radioactive materials with a higher curie content. They must meet all Type A standards and be able to withstand a severe accident without the loss of shielding or the release of radioactive materials.

Special shipping casks for spent fuel are even more elaborate and rugged. (Solidified high-level waste will be shipped in similar heavily shielded casks, which are still in the conceptual design stage.) These casks for shipping spent fuel generally consist of a stainless steel cylinder with a heavy metal shield, enclosed in a steel shell. The casks are designed to withstand a sequence of hypothetical tests that encompass a range of very severe accident conditions, including impact, puncture, fire, and immersion in water without releasing more than a specified small amount of radioactive material. (It should be noted that analytical methods, rather than actual field tests on sample casks, are used to assess the ability of a cask design to pass these tests.)

To date, most accidents and leakages in transit have involved low-level wastes, and no deaths or serious injuries have been traced to them. In fact, compared to transport of other hazardous materials, radioactive shipments have an excellent record. But, questions continue to be raised about packaging requirements and the tests. Critics point out that some accidents involve higher speeds than those involved in the thirty-foot drop test and that some actual fires are hotter than the temperatures assumed in the tests. Furthermore, they emphasize that no actual casks have been field-tested, that nine of the seventeen casks in existence have at one time been withdrawn from service because of defects,[7] and that the Nuclear Regulatory Commission lacks adequate staff to do periodic checks on all packaging.

The Congressional Office of Technology Assessment in its 1985 report, *Managing the Nation's Commercial High-Level Radioactive Waste*, summed up the debate over transportation safety in these words:

> Review of the debate about transportation safety did not reveal any fundamental technical challenges to the conclusion that shipping casks can be designed to prevent significant radioactive releases in realistic accident conditions. At the same time, it is clear that the central role of shipping cask integrity in providing transportation safety places considerable importance on ensuring that great care is taken in the manufacture, testing, use, and maintenance of casks.[8]

Routing

The route of a radioactive material shipment depends on the type of material in the shipment, its size, the distance it must travel, and federal, state, and local regulations.

The U.S. Department of Transportation issued two sets of routing regulations in 1981 for highway carriers of radioactive materials. First, there is a general set of regulations governing the radioactive shipments of radiopharmaceuticals, industrial isotopes, and low-level wastes which, if properly packaged, are considered to present relatively minimal risks compared to other hazardous materials such as gasoline. These regulations allow carriers to use their own discretion in selecting routes. The second set of routing rules, which applies to motor vehicles transporting large quantities of radioactive materials, is more stringent. Carriers are required to use interstate highways as preferred routes, to avoid urban centers by using bypasses and beltways when available, to avoid travel during rush hours, and to avoid local hazards such as roads and bridges under construction or repair. Furthermore, drivers must have special driver training certification and be notified that they are carrying radioactive materials.

Many state and local governments have established their own rules, specifying such things as prenotification requirements, time-of-day restrictions, routes, and special equipment. The most recent example is the April 1985 ordinance enacted by the Denver City Council. In addition to many of the above requirements, the Denver law levies a fee on hazardous and radioactive waste shipments within the city. The fees will be used to underwrite costs of administration and emergency response.

Some state and local governments have adopted bans on the transport of nuclear waste through their jurisdictions. In 1976 New York City authorities banned shipments of large quantities of radioactive materials and spent nuclear fuel through the city. When the Department of Transportation issued its 1981 regulations allowing preemption (i.e., overriding) of local restrictions, the city of New York immediately sued to block the regulations. A federal district court sided with New York City in a very narrowly written ruling, agreeing that, in the case of New York City, DOT's environmental appraisal and assumptions about a "worst case scenario" were inadequate. The U.S. Circuit Court of Appeals overturned that decision, and in February 1984 the Supreme Court refused to hear the case, leaving the DOT regulations intact. The decision upholds the authority of federal regulation but allows state and local governments to petition DOT for a waiver of the regulations.

The Department of Transportation asserts that state and local rules are, in many cases, conflicting and that they restrict interstate commerce. State agencies may designate alternative preferred routes under the DOT routing rule, but the agency maintains that state and local regulations that unnecessarily burden, delay, or ban shipments will be preempted under the Hazardous Materials Transportation Act. It seems likely that this controversy, pitting the rights of states and local governments against the authority of the federal government, will continue to be aired in the courts.

LIABILITY COVERAGE FOR ACCIDENTS

The passage of the Nuclear Waste Policy Act of 1982 has heightened concern not only about the increased shipments of radioactive waste but also about the adequacy of liability coverage for such shipments.

Currently, liability for a nuclear accident—whether it occurs at a nuclear power plant, a Department of Energy facility, or along a transportation route—is determined by the provisions of the Price-Anderson Act. This amendment to the 1954 Atomic Energy Act has two purposes: to ensure compensation for the public in the case of a nuclear accident and to protect the nuclear industry from a potential accident liability so large that it would threaten the future of nuclear power.

First passed in 1957 and renewed for ten years in 1966 and again in 1975, Price-Anderson sets up a two-tier "no-fault" system of insurance against accidents at nuclear power plants, with a current $605 million ceiling. A utility buys the first layer of insurance—$160 million—from private insurance firms. The second layer is a pool fund into which each utility is obliged to put up to $5 million per *operating* nuclear reactor. In 1984, that pool fund totaled $425 million, since there were eighty-five operating reactors. In exchange for this limited liability, the Price-Anderson Act imposes what is known as "strict liability" on the utility involved in an accident that is determined by the NRC to be an "extraordinary nuclear occurrence" (ENO). Strict liability means that the utility must waive normal legal defenses against paying claims (up to the ceiling), relieving victims from proving that the utility was negligent or "at fault." To recover damages under this provision, affected citizens need only show that their losses were caused by the extraordinary nuclear occurrence.

In the event of an accident involving the transportation of nuclear waste, the amount of funds available for public compensation and the source of those funds turn on whether the particular shipment falls under the jurisdiction of NRC-licensees (commercial nuclear power plants) or under Department of Energy contractors.

A shipping accident involving NRC licensees would be treated like an accident at a nuclear power plant, with a total potential compensation of $605 million. These provisions cover all shipments of nuclear material *to* or *from* nuclear power plants, including enriched fuel sent to a power plant, spent fuel transported to a storage or disposal facility, and low-level waste shipped to a disposal site.

Shipping accidents involving companies operating under contracts with the Department of Energy are insured directly by the federal government. The Department of Energy, in effect, executes an indemnity agreement with the contractor to cover up to $500 million in damages. Shipments in this category include (1) high-level waste transported from one storage facility to another, to a disposal site or to a repository; (2) spent fuel or low-level waste from government, research, or foreign reactors en route to storage, to a repository, or to disposal facilities; (3) enriched uranium hexafluoride shipped from an enrichment plant to a fuel fabrication plant; (4) nonirradiated fuel shipped from a fuel fabrication facility to a federal government or research reactor; and (5) uranium hexafluoride transported from a conversion facility to an enrichment plant.

Should the NRC or DOE determine that a transportation accident is an "extraordinary nuclear occurrence," then the "strict liability" provision, described above, would come into play. Thus far, no accident warranting this designation has occurred.

Since the Price-Anderson Act will expire in 1987, hearings are now under way in Congress to consider whether the act should be extended beyond 1987 and, if so, whether there should be any changes in the present coverage. Both DOE and NRC have submitted reports to Congress urging its extension with some proposed changes. Among the issues that Congress is expected to consider are the limit on liability; coverage in the event of sabotage or theft of nuclear materials during transportation; a state or local government's ability to recover expenses related to precautionary evacuation or emergency response costs; and whether state or local governments are liable for accidents due to poorly maintained bridges and roads in their jurisdictions.

5

The Politics of Radioactive Waste Management

▼   ▼   ▼   ▼   ▼

Decisions about how to provide for permanent disposal of low-level nuclear waste will be made by states—singly or in regional groupings. Decisions about permanent disposal of high-level waste, including spent fuel, will be made by the federal government, with state and Indian tribe involvement. And although there is agreement about much of the scientific basis for safe disposal of nuclear waste, there is much less agreement about the development and implementation of disposal plans.

Debates over waste disposal—whether for low-level or high-level wastes—are conducted on both a scientific-technical level and a political–public policy level. The debate over *high-level waste* began with discussions among technical experts about the best type of disposal method. Then after a basic consensus emerged in favor of geologic disposal, further divisions of opinion cropped up. Which kind of geologic formation is best? Which site is best suited for isolating the waste? These technical questions in turn became the basis for political policy disputes. And whenever a specific site is identified as being potentially suitable as a permanent nuclear waste repository, state and local concerns open another round of controversy.

The current debate on *low-level waste* begins with the political questions (How shall regional groupings of states be formed? In which state will the facility be located?). The focus then moves on to the technical (What kind of a facility? What type of site?) and returns to the political (Why here?).

It is not surprising that people want the benefits of medical research and treatment, electric power generation, and manufacturing processes without the worry or risk of coping with the "nuclear leftovers." Neither is it surprising that federal and state officials want to make decisions without continual reopening of the debate or last-minute second guessing by anxious citizens or other officials. However, the political decision-making framework must allow all participants to play their parts fully and effectively. Citizens and state and local governments are rightful participants—along with the federal government—in decision-making about nuclear power and radioactive waste management. Clearly, one result of the process must be a public perception, solidly based in reality, that the risks have been assessed with care and candor and that burdens have been shared equitably.

The political issues and the tools for resolving waste-disposal issues are discussed in this chapter. The next chapter outlines the array of technical opinion.

HIGH-LEVEL WASTE MANAGEMENT

From the development of nuclear technology until 1982 the search for a scientifically, technically, and politically acceptable system for managing high-level waste and spent reactor fuel was in a continual state of flux. In 1974 the Atomic Energy Commission—the agency originally in charge—was dismantled and its responsibilities were divided among other federal agencies. The Nuclear Regulatory Commission took over regulatory functions and the Energy Research and Development Administration handled research and development. In the fall of 1977 the Energy Research and Development Administration was subsumed under the newly created Department of Energy, which has since undergone several major internal reorganizations.

Meanwhile, many of the basic elements of the high-level waste-management scheme—temporary storage (at reactors? away from reactors? federally or utility owned?), reprocessing (economically feasible? technically required? politically wise?), long-term storage (technically desirable? or serving only to delay decisions?), and disposal (how? where? chosen by what criteria?)—were constantly shifting as administrations, agencies, and personnel changed. At the same time, policies governing who could actually participate in decision-making also varied. Not surprisingly, both officials and citizens have had great difficulty in following these developments and in feeling confident about management processes and decisions.

Since late 1982, however, a number of elements of the picture have become clearer. Although many issues have yet to be resolved, the Nuclear Waste Policy Act passed by Congress in December 1982 provides a framework for making decisions and assigns responsibility for implementing them.

The Nuclear Waste Policy Act:

sets a schedule for the siting, construction, and operation of high-level waste repositories;

defines the working and decision-making relationships between the federal government, state governments, and Indian tribes;

establishes federal policy and responsibility for nuclear waste management;

requires the establishment of a fund to cover nuclear waste disposal costs.

Geologic Repository Development

With the signing of the Nuclear Waste Policy Act by President Reagan in January 1983, the Department of Energy faced a number of tasks to be completed under a very demanding schedule mandated by the Congress. The most pressing was the requirement to develop, by July 1983, guidelines for selecting a geologic high-level repository site. The department set out to meet that deadline and by February 1983 had issued draft-siting guidelines and launched a series of five public hearings across the country. What officials heard was, "You're moving too fast." Citizens, state officials, and other federal agencies made it clear that they could not respond adequately on such short notice and charged the Department of Energy with insensitivity to public concerns. As a result, the Department of Energy switched gears and began a slower, more deliberate process involving the states and other federal agencies in a consultative process.

The siting guidelines are now in force as regulations, and the Department of Energy is using them as the basis for evaluating and recommending sites for further study. However, the controversy has not entirely ended. Several lawsuits have been initiated by a number of interested parties, including environmental organizations and states. They are challenging the guidelines and the decision process in force to date.

The lesson that the Department of Energy has learned from this experience—that public policy develops at its own pace and that it is imprudent, or even impossible, to proceed too quickly—should guide future procedures and decisions. The schedule mandated by the act is now regarded as more flexible, although the Department of Energy still maintains that it will be prepared to accept spent fuel from utilities in 1998 as mandated by the Nuclear Waste Policy Act. However, some critics still fear that adherence to that commitment may shift the emphasis from reaching sound solutions to adhering strictly to the timetable.

First Repository   In 1975 the Energy Research and Development Administration began a search for possible permanent repository sites. The first undertaking in this effort was a multiple-site survey of underground geologic formations in thirty-six states. This screening, which continued under the Department of Energy, was reduced in scope due to political opposition from states and to reduced funding. The search for sites in bedded salt was narrowed to the Paradox Basin in Utah and the Permian Basin in New Mexico and Texas. The search for domed salt sites was narrowed to the interior Gulf Coast region. The Department of Energy also looked for promising sites on land already owned by the government and dedicated to nuclear use. This led to consideration of one location in basalt—a fine-grained igneous rock—on the Hanford Reservation near Richland, Washington, and one in tuff—a rock formed of compacted volcanic ash and dust—at Yucca Mountain on the Nevada Test Site.

In February 1983 the Department of Energy formally identified nine sites in five distinct geohydrologic settings as potentially ac-

Figure 12. Nine potentially acceptable sites for first geologic respository for high-level waste. *U.S. Department of Energy*

ceptable for a mined geologic repository for spent nuclear fuel and high-level radioactive waste. Hearings were held in each of the six affected states—Louisiana, Mississippi, Nevada, Texas, Utah, and Washington. The Department of Energy next prepared an environmental assessment (EA) for each site. The goal was first to nominate five of the sites for possible site characterization (in-depth studies and data collection at the site, including the actual drilling of an exploratory shaft) and then to recommend three of those sites to the President for actual characterization. Critics charge that these steps are premature and argue that the Nuclear Waste Policy Act requires the Department of Energy to undertake a new full-scale screening process rather than to proceed with sites already under consideration prior to passage of the act. There is further disagreement about whether the act requires the site characterization process to be *undertaken* at only three sites—the Department of Energy position—or that the characterization process *result* in the identification of three suitable sites.

Draft environmental assessments, issued in December 1984, stated that each of the nine sites was "not disqualified under the guidelines." Further, the assessments concluded that all of the sites are suitable for site characterization because "the evidence does not support a conclusion that the site will not be able to meet each of the qualifying conditions specified in the guidelines."

In its draft environmental assessments, the Department of Energy proposed the nomination of sites at Hanford, Washington, Yucca Mountain, Nevada, Deaf Smith County, Texas, Davis Canyon, Utah, and Richton Dome, Mississippi, as the top five sites for a mined geologic repository and recommended that of these five, the Nevada, Texas, and Washington sites be chosen for characterization as possible first repositories. Under terms of the act, sites ranked four and five (in this case Davis Canyon, Utah, and Richton Dome, Mississippi) and not chosen to be characterized may not be considered for the second repository (see below), although those with lower rankings on the current list may be.

When the Secretary of Energy recommends three sites to the President for site characterization, the President may (1) approve or disapprove the recommendations within 60 days, or (2) formally delay the decision by not more than six months to gather further information.

If the President fails to act in the prescribed time, the recommendations of the Secretary of Energy stand.

The preparation of a site characterization plan for each of the three sites will then be initiated. Each plan must be submitted to the affected state or Indian tribe and to the Nuclear Regulatory Commission before an exploratory shaft can be constructed. Once the characterization process is complete (a task expected to take approximately five years), the Department of Energy will evaluate each site against its siting guidelines, prepare an environmental impact statement, and recommend one site to the President for the first permanent nuclear waste repository. The recommendation will include comments from the Nuclear Regulatory Commission, the host state, and any affected Indian tribes. The President must then recommend the final site to Congress. At that time, the host state or affected Indian tribe may issue a notice of disapproval. That "veto" will stand unless overridden by a joint resolution of Congress.

Once a repository site has been designated, the Department of Energy must submit an application to the Nuclear Regulatory Commission for construction authorization. The commission must make a decision on the application within three years, with a one-year extension possible.

Second Repository The Nuclear Waste Policy Act of 1982 also requires the Department of Energy to identify a site for a second high-level waste repository. Although the act does not authorize construction of a second repository, it does limit the amount of waste that can be placed in the first repository before a second one begins operation. The search for a second site now centers on granite formations in seventeen eastern and midwestern states: Connecticut, Georgia, Maine, Maryland, Massachusetts, Michigan, Minnesota, New Hampshire, New Jersey, New York, North Carolina, Pennsylvania, Rhode Island, South Carolina, Vermont, Virginia, and Wisconsin.

This second search has profited from the lessons learned during the first. A nationwide screening process first identified regions that might contain suitable sites. Next, the search will be narrowed from multistate regions to smaller areas using a method developed with extensive consultation between the Department of Energy and the affected states. Identification of areas to receive further study was scheduled for early 1986. Then the Department of Energy will investigate the chosen areas in greater detail, further narrow the search to specific sites, and follow the procedure outlined under the first repository process to develop a recommendation for a second repository site.

State/Federal Relations

Relations have been less than tranquil between the federal government and states that either contain identified sites or feel they may be next on the list. No states have expressed interest in furnishing a site for a permanent high-level waste (and spent fuel) repository. In fact, more than a dozen states, responding to pressure from citizens, have enacted laws intended to either flatly prohibit or make difficult the establishment within their borders of disposal facilities for either high-level waste or low-level radioactive waste. And a Nuclear Regulatory Commission survey reports that more are considering following suit.

Why do so many state and local governments want to restrict or prohibit nuclear waste disposal (and even temporary storage) within their boundaries? One reason is that adverse experiences with other projects involving hazardous substances have made states wary of possible future problems connected to the siting of nuclear waste facilities within their borders. Citizens and state and local officials want assurances that the facilities will be properly managed now and in the future and that they will pose no significant risks to people or to the environment.

In western states, where suitable geology, dry climate, and sparse population combine to create favorable conditions for nuclear waste disposal, many state officials are in an especially mutinous mood. These states have been the sites for many federally sponsored hazardous activities in the past, including above-ground atomic bomb tests, uranium mining, milling and tailings disposal, and nerve gas production, testing, and storage. Often these remote locations were selected to minimize the risk to the population at large. But as one westerner put it, "The government has used the wide open spaces as a dumping ground for almost four decades and inflicted a lot of wounds on us. Well, we've just had enough." On the other hand, some people living near potential sites are eager for the economic benefits they feel a repository will bring.

Congress recognized the potentially troublesome problem of federal/state relations in the Nuclear Waste Policy Act. The law gives states and affected Indian tribes a formal role in reviewing the site selection process and authorizes federal funding for state oversight of the Department of Energy waste-site research programs. Finally, the act permits the host state to issue a notice of disapproval when the President recommends a repository site to Congress. As noted above, that "veto" can only be overridden by a joint resolution of both Houses of Congress.

One operating model for a productive state/federal working relationship emerged during the development of the Waste Isolation Pilot Plant (WIPP) for disposal of defense-related transuranic waste at Carlsbad, New Mexico. Litigation by the state resulted in an agreement guaranteeing federal "consultation and cooperation" between the Department of Energy and the state of New Mexico regarding the health and safety aspects of the project. New Mexico's Environmental Evaluation Group, an independent state government agency funded by the U.S. Department of Energy, monitors the development of the WIPP repository, providing oversight for the state. Several other states, most notably Wisconsin, have enacted legislation setting up procedures for state involvement and oversight of federal radioactive waste-management programs.

Federal Policy and Responsibility

In addition to mandating the construction of one geologic repository by 1998 and the siting of a second, the Nuclear Waste Policy Act defined the process for making decisions about other elements of a high-level nuclear waste management system. It also established the Office of Civilian Radioactive Waste Management, in the Department of Energy, to implement the act.

Further, the Nuclear Waste Policy Act mandates that the Office of Civilian Radioactive Waste Management prepare and deliver a "mission plan" to Congress. That plan, issued in June 1985, discusses the current and predicted amounts of high-level nuclear waste to be managed, the data base required by the Department of Energy to make decisions about various elements of the program, and a research agenda for assembling that information. The Department of Energy views the "mission plan" as a working document that will be reviewed and updated periodically.

The act also requires a study by the Department of Energy on the need for and feasibility of a facility for the long-term storage of high-level waste (called monitored retrievable storage or MRS). In April 1985, the Department of Energy issued a study that recommended consideration of three sites in Tennessee for a monitored retrievable storage facility and construction of one MRS as part of an integrated waste-management system. Such a facility would receive spent fuel from commercial power reactors, consolidate and package the spent fuel, and then store the fuel temporarily pending shipment to a repository. The facility is envisioned as a receiving and handling facility to complement a repository rather than as a backup to a repository. It would be centrally located near the majority of reactors, and DOE argues that the impact of transportation to the final disposal facility would be minimized by shipping spent fuel in large rail casks on "dedicated unit" trains used only to transport this cargo.

On another issue, the Nuclear Waste Policy Act requires that the Department of Energy assess alternative ways of managing the civilian waste-management program. A committee appointed by the secretary of the Department of Energy recommended that an independent, federally chartered corporation be set up to manage the civilian nuclear waste program. However, an internal Department of Energy review committee rejected that proposal and concluded that the present structure (the Office of Civilian Radioactive Waste Management) should be retained, at least through the siting and licensing stages.

In addition, the act gave the Department of Energy two other responsibilities—to develop transportation and interim storage plans and to make a final recommendation about whether defense waste should be disposed of in civilian repositories. DOE issued a draft transportation "business plan" in July 1985. In April 1985, the President accepted the department's recommendation to dispose of defense waste in civilian repositories.

When all these reports and plans are completed and decisions are made about their implementation, the outline of an integrated nuclear waste management system should emerge.

Waste Fund

The Nuclear Waste Fund, provided for in the Nuclear Waste Policy Act, is supported by user fees intended to fully underwrite the costs of the Department of Energy disposal programs mandated in the legislation. The fund, based on the principle that users of the electrical power generated by nuclear energy should bear the cost of disposal of the resulting radioactive waste, assesses two kinds of fees: (1) a one-time charge per kilogram of heavy metal in high-level waste or spent fuel in existence before April 1983; and (2) an adjustable fee, initially one mill per kilowatt hour, levied on electricity generated by nuclear reactors after April 1983. This fee is subject to annual review and adjustments to be certain it covers all costs.

LOW-LEVEL WASTE MANAGEMENT

The Low-Level Radioactive Waste Policy Act, passed by Congress in December 1980, established two major national policies: (1) Each state is responsible for assuring adequate disposal capacity for the low-level waste generated within its own borders, with the exception of waste generated by federal defense or research and development activities. (2) The required disposal facilities can best be provided through regional groupings of states allied through interstate agreements called compacts. A compact ratified by a group of states must be approved by Congress before it takes full effect. Consent to a compact may be withdrawn by Congress every five years.

Congress added an incentive to states to work together, stipulating that any regional compact may include a provision to exclude waste from outside the region's borders after January 1, 1986.

The act did not designate specific regional groupings, and therefore much of the action since its passage has centered on state decisions about whether and which region to join and negotiations among states to form compact regions and establish formal compact agreements. States found that their concerns and choices varied with their own particular situations.

States with currently operating low-level waste disposal sites (Nevada, South Carolina, and Washington) had to decide whether to allow those sites to continue operating after January 1986—and if so, whether to propose them as regional disposal sites. States that generate high volumes of waste but have no operating disposal site consider it likely that they will be targeted to host sites in any regional grouping. Consequently, they want to retain enough control over decisions so that a proposed facility would meet both their state environmental standards and disposal requirements. States that generate little waste fear that membership in a compact would force them to become dumping grounds for neighboring states' high volumes of waste.

In short, all states are concerned about assuring adequate protection for their interests if they choose to join a compact.

Not surprisingly, the regions that include currently operating

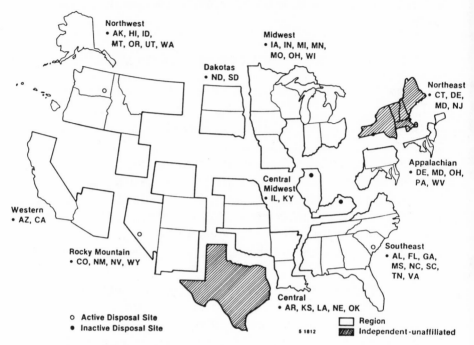

Figure 13. Low-level radioactive waste compact status. *U.S. Department of Energy*

commercial low-level disposal sites—the Southeast and the Northwest—reached agreement most easily. The major stumbling blocks for other potential regional groupings are deciding how to choose a host state and how to share liability for a site failure or accident.

As states commit themselves to various solutions, the outline of a slightly unwieldy national system of regional groupings emerges (see Figure 13). Compact agreements have been reached among states in the Northwest, Rocky Mountain, Midwest, Central, and Southeast regions and have been introduced in Congress. Texas has decided to go it alone, develop its own site, and rely on legal means other than a compact to reserve its capacity for exclusive Texas use. The major-generator states of California and Illinois plan to host disposal sites and rely on a compact with a neighboring small-generator state—Arizona and Kentucky, respectively—to ensure that they will be able to exclude out-of-region waste. In the Northeast, where many of the large waste-generating states are located, compact groupings remain unsettled, although Pennsylvania has taken the lead in moving toward a compact with adjoining states.

Figure 14. Production of low-level waste, by state, as of 1983 (latest available figures). This table, which shows the volume of wastes and amount of radio-activity shipped in commercial disposal sites, is based on disposal site records. *The Radioactive Exchange*

State	Volume (m³)	Radioactivity (curies)
Alabama	4,360	8,055
Alaska	0	0
Arizona	0	0
Arkansas	790	2,056
California	3,781	41,518
Colorado	71	21
Connecticut	1,890	2,469
Delaware	30	2
District of Columbia	98	2
Florida	2,418	95,046
Georgia	1,950	2,699
Hawaii	130	10
Idaho	0	0
Illinois	6,196	13,773
Indiana	20	5
Iowa	724	1,424
Kansas	0	0
Kentucky	74	5
Louisiana	16	3
Maine	342	103
Maryland	1,342	212
Massachusetts	4,726	77,402
Michigan	1,542	27,909
Minnesota	1,259	44,714
Mississippi	427	7
Missouri	230	1,016
Montana	2	0
Nebraska	922	1,402
Nevada	0	0
New Hampshire	63	1
New Jersey	3,633	1,567
New Mexico	39	7
New York	5,622	70,192
North Carolina	4,698	6,160
North Dakota	0	0
Ohio	807	5,000
Oklahoma	64	700
Oregon	1,394	1,691
Pennsylvania	7,658	23,989
Puerto Rico	0	0
Rhode Island	53	0
South Carolina	5,600	4,160
South Dakota	0	0
Tennessee	4,506	2,994
Texas	1,628	1,547
Utah	87	11
Vermont	637	57,174
Virginia	4,718	5,768
Washington	1,279	2,538
West Virginia	20	0
Wisconsin	784	1,988
Wyoming	0	0
Total	76,702	503,340

The principal drawback to this emerging system is the large number of individual states and regions that propose to build new disposal facilities; ultimately this may provide more capacity than is economically viable.

It is clear that no new disposal capacity will be available by 1986 since it takes approximately five years to site, license, and construct a facility. Nevertheless, citizens in Nevada, South Carolina, and Washington want Congress to honor the intent of the Low-Level Radioactive Waste Policy Act and allow them to exclude out-of-region waste from their disposal sites in 1986. A tentative compromise on the issue was reached in July 1985 when the House Interior and Insular Affairs Committee approved legislation that eases the deadlines for states to develop disposal facilities. The compromise allows the January 1, 1986 deadline to be moved back to December 31, 1992, as long as waste-producing states are meeting a timetable for developing new sites within their own compacts. The bill sets a series of "milestones" to cut off access to any state not meeting them.

The same committee also recommended giving congressional consent to six compacts—the Northwest, Central, Southeast, Central Midwest, Midwest, and Rocky Mountains regions.

Making decisions about the disposal of nuclear waste has not been easy at any level of government. Some wonder why we can't get on with it without so much political fuss. But in a representative democracy citizens have a right to be involved in decision-making. The challenge is to find ways to make sound scientific decisions that are also publicly acceptable.

6

The Search for a Permanent Solution

▼   ▼   ▼   ▼   ▼

No matter how much political skill is brought to the complex decisions about nuclear waste disposal, the successful long-term isolation of radionuclides from the environment will depend on scientific understanding and technical and managerial competence.

HIGH-LEVEL WASTES

Geologic Disposal

The shorthand term "geologic disposal" refers to permanent disposal of nuclear waste in a stable, deep geologic (rock) formation. The disposal area, or repository, to be carved out of rock at least one thousand feet below ground, will be designed to contain and isolate the high-level radioactive waste using a combination of natural features and man-made components. Together they will provide a series of barriers to the release of radionuclides into the environment: the chemical form of the waste; the canister that

61

holds the waste; any packing material around the canister; and finally, the rock formation itself.

The concept of geologic disposal of high-level waste/spent fuel and transuranic waste has theoretical acceptance, at least, in much of the scientific community. A recent study by the National Academy of Sciences concludes that although technology is not yet far enough advanced to completely design, construct, and operate such a repository, current research *can* serve as a basis for the next steps, which should lead both to the selection of candidate sites for in-situ testing and to the development of the needed expertise for subsequent steps.[9]

Geologic disposal has been the focus of federal research for more than thirty years. A 1957 National Academy of Sciences report, commissioned by the Atomic Energy Commission, recommended the burial of high-level and transuranic waste in geologic formations. The academy urged the investigation of a large number of potential sites and specifically recommended further research on salt beds and salt domes. Since salt is highly soluble, the very existence of salt formations indicates that they are generally free of cracks through which water or brine could travel. This fact constitutes a major advantage to disposal in salt, because the principal means for radionuclides to escape from a geologic repository is in water that flows through cracks—either to the surface or into groundwater.

Salt formations have another important advantage. Since salt creeps under heat and pressure, any fractures in the formation resulting from tectonic activity eventually heal themselves. In addition, the persistence of salt deposits for 200 million years or more demonstrates their stability.

However, investigators have identified some potential problems with the use of salt formations for nuclear waste disposal. Over thousands of years, groundwater *has* in some cases penetrated and altered some salt formations in ways that are difficult to detect from the surface and are not yet fully understood. Furthermore, very small (often microscopic) inclusions of brine have been found in both salt beds and domes. If the radioactive decay of the wastes generated sufficient heat to cause these brine inclusions to rupture, the brine could conceivably contact and corrode the waste packages. The fact that salt formations often exist close to other underground natural resources such as natural gas, oil, and gypsum is also a potential problem. Part of the debate about the building of the Waste Isolation Pilot Plant (WIPP) repository in salt beds near Carlsbad in southeastern New Mexico centered on the commercial gas deposits that lie below the salt beds and the potash deposits that lie above.

These lingering questions about salt formations may be answered by research being conducted at the Waste Isolation Pilot Project. The WIPP site was originally chosen by the Energy Research and Development Administration (a Department of Energy predecessor) in 1975 as a successor to the project abandoned at Lyons, Kansas, for disposal of defense transuranic wastes. Over the past decade, the project has gone through many metamorphoses including changes in purpose and attempts to cancel altogether a project at that site. WIPP has now emerged in a form similar to its original one: a facility for the disposal of transuranic wastes generated in United States defense programs and for research using a small quantity of high-level defense waste. As such, the facility is not subject to licensing by the Nuclear Regulatory Commission. Already more than ten thousand feet of tunnels, or drifts, have been mined twenty-five hundred feet underground, and experiments at repository depths are under way. If all goes well, the facility will become a permanent repository for transuranic wastes. The high-level wastes will be removed from WIPP at the conclusion of the tests.[10]

In addition to investigating salt domes and beds, the Department of Energy also is actively conducting research on geologic formations of basalt, tuff, and crystalline rock (granite) as potential nuclear waste disposal sites. Shale, alluvium, and argillite formations have also been considered. Unlike salt, these types of geologic formations are always fractured to some degree. If these cracks are connected to one another, groundwater can pass through the rock. But these rock formations, unlike salt, have the ability to chemically adsorb most waste elements. Thus, if moving groundwater were to leach wastes from a repository and carry it toward aquifers or toward the surface, the ability of the rock to adsorb radionuclides would retard transport and help prevent the contamination of water supplies.

To learn more about the interaction of these rock formations with radioactive wastes, the Department of Energy has conducted experiments in basalt at the Hanford Reservation in Washington and in granite, shale, and other kinds of rock formations at the Nevada Test Site. The Department of Energy also is participating in related international research projects, most notably in Canada, Sweden, and the Federal Republic of Germany (see What Other Countries Are Doing, page 70).

If nuclear wastes are buried underground in salt or other rock formations, what are the odds that groundwater might leach radionuclides from the wastes and carry them to the environment in health-threatening concentrations? Clearly, that is the bottom-line question. Most studies to date suggest that, in a properly sited repository, the odds are very low. The 1983 National Academy of Sciences study—*A Study of the Isolation System for Geologic Disposal of Radioactive Waste*—concluded that it is possible to identify repository rock bodies from which it would take several thousands to millions of years for a drop of water to travel from the repository to the biosphere—long enough for significant containment in the geologic material and decay of most of the radionuclides to take place.

Of course, there are other potential ways in which radionuclides might be released into the environment that must be considered in estimating the risks associated with a potential repository site. For example, radionuclides could be released by human activity such as exploratory drilling or attempts to recover some natural resource thought to lie in the vicinity of the repository. Some of the Department of Energy siting guidelines and procedures, as well as research projects investigating alternative materials and methods, are designed to decrease the risk of such occurrences.

Experts cite the "Oklo" phenomenon as convincing evidence in favor of disposing of high-level waste in stable geologic formations. Two billion years ago, natural events operating on a very rich uranium deposit in what is now Gabon, in Africa, led to nuclear fission reactions. This "natural" nuclear reactor produced the same types of wastes as man-made reactors. Studies of the site (near a village called Oklo) show that most of the fission products and virtually all the transuranic elements, including plutonium, have moved less than six feet from where they were formed 20 million centuries ago.

Other Kinds of Permanent Disposal

While disposal deep within geologic formations has dominated both scientific and policy discussions, other methods of disposal of high-level wastes have been considered. Indeed, the Nuclear Waste Policy Act requires the Department of Energy to research alternative technologies for the permanent disposal of high-level waste.

Currently the only alternative actively being researched is disposal under deep-sea sediments. In a program that began in 1973, the United States, in cooperation with several other countries, is investigating the feasibility of burying waste packages in geologic formations beneath the deep ocean floor. Current research is focusing on areas in international waters (more than two hundred miles from shore) in the western North Pacific and the North Atlantic where the ocean is three thousand to five thousand meters deep, the sea floor is flat, and the sediments are thick and uniform over a large area. These areas are very stable geologically, virtually bereft of life, and isolated from the rest of the planet. Sediments in these areas consist of extremely fine-grained clay that will adsorb most of the radionuclides in the wastes. They are considered the primary barrier to the release of radionuclides into the biosphere.

Research thus far has not revealed any major flaws in the subseabed concept, but important technical questions remain to be answered; they include the rate at which water flows, if indeed it moves at all, through ocean sediments and the potential effect of the heat generated by waste packages on the surrounding sediment. The United States research project plans to report on the feasibility of the subseabed concept in the 1990s. Whatever its technical merits, the proposal will face significant institutional hurdles such as amendment of United States and international law.

Several other suggested alternatives, which now appear to be impractical, have been put on the back burner. One suggestion was to bury canisters of waste in the Antarctic ice sheet. However, this suggestion has been abandoned because the stability of the ice caps over the thousands of years required for the radioactive decay of the wastes is highly uncertain. Similarly, the idea of rocketing nuclear waste into space, although ruled technically feasible by the National Aeronautics and Space Administration in the early 1970s, is no longer under investigation because both the cost and the risk of a launch accident are considered to be too high.

It also has been proposed that high-level waste be bombarded with neutrons inside a reactor and transmuted into shorter-lived or less harmful substances. Unfortunately, existing fission reactors do not do a very good job of altering cesium-137 or strontium-90, two of the most hazardous waste components, and the cost and complexity of separating each waste nuclide for such treatment is too great for practical consideration.

Some people have argued that we can safely delay answering the question of how and where to dispose of wastes for fifty years or longer. They recommend keeping spent fuel rods or canisters of solidified high-level waste in deepwater pools or storing them above ground in air-cooled casks or vaults, maintaining continuous human surveillance until the radioactivity and heat given off by the short-lived nuclides in these wastes have decreased to more manageable levels. It would take about three hundred years of such storage for the wastes to cool down to the temperature of their surroundings. Sweden and France, for example, have incorporated long-term storage as an element of their waste disposal plans.

Proponents of long-term storage for the United States point out that such a plan would buy more time for the development of disposal options. But others, including some critics of the government's past track record on nuclear waste management, see this proposal as a delaying tactic and say that now is the time to develop a permanent solution—before this country makes further commitments to nuclear power.

Waste Form—What Shall We Bury?

Department of Energy planners are now designing the nation's commercial disposal system based on the permanent isolation of spent fuel rods since, as noted earlier, spent fuel is currently not being reprocessed in this country (see Reprocessing, page 14). The government also must plan for disposal of federal high-level waste from defense activities.

Almost all strategies for disposal of high-level waste presuppose that the liquid and sludge will be solidified into a glass or a ceramic form and sealed into metal canisters before being disposed of in a geologic formation. Spent fuel is already in ceramic form and thus would not need to undergo the solidification step. Just as bedded salt has been considered for many years to be the most suitable geologic formation for waste disposal, incorporation into glass (vitrification) has long been considered the best way to immobilize high-level wastes before disposal. Some studies have shown, however, that while radionuclides leach to a certain extent from all solid waste forms when they are in contact with water over long periods of time, the leach rate of borosilicate glass is greatly accelerated by high temperatures and steam—thermal stress conditions that are to be expected in the fresh high-level waste. This problem can be alleviated either by increasing the dilution of the radioactive material in the glass or by cooling the high-level waste for several years before vitrification. These procedures would lower the amount of heat the glass would have to endure and prevent the formation of steam.

A 1979 report by the National Academy of Sciences concluded that although glass may be suitable for use in a waste solidification and disposal system, it is generally less stable than crystalline materials such as ceramics and it may not be the ultimate preferred waste form. The study suggested that other waste forms should be evaluated for use over the long term. Spent fuel, which already is a ceramic, has been shown in some studies to have a lower leachability rate than some formulations of glass.

At present, the biggest advantage of glass is that glass-making technology is far more advanced than the technology for ceramics. High-level wastes can be added to glass and formed into large blocks, whereas ceramic processing is being done only in the laboratory. France, with a reprocessing system already in place, is operating a glass plant at Marcoule designed to handle all the waste produced in that country's nuclear facilities. Marcoule also processes waste from several other countries.

As was the case in the United States until Presidents Ford and Carter changed U.S. policy, the nuclear waste disposal plans of most other countries are predicated on the reprocessing of spent fuel (see What Other Countries Are Doing, page 70). However, while it is true that recycling spent fuel does extend fuel resources, some experts question the desirability of reprocessing simply as a step in the waste-management system. They point out that spent fuel is already a ceramic; hence, one difficult step in dealing with high-level wastes is obviated. There is certainly more complexity, and thus greater risk, in reprocessing spent fuel and solidifying the resultant liquid high-level waste than in directly disposing of spent fuel. While the high-level waste left over after spent fuel is reprocessed does contain a smaller amount of extremely long-lived transuranics than does spent fuel, reprocessing produces an additional volume of wastes contaminated with transuranic radionuclides.

Another issue that has been the subject of debate is how long nuclear waste should be retrievable from a repository. Current Nuclear Regulatory Commission regulations require that waste be retrievable for fifty years, with no greater difficulty than excavating the repository in the first place, in case problems develop.

LOW-LEVEL WASTES

While some low-level waste has been disposed of at sea, particularly during the 1950s, most has been disposed of in shallow land burial sites. Typically, these wastes are separated according to type of packaging required and degree of hazard; the containerized waste is then placed in trenches. The dimensions of these trenches vary with the soil and water conditions of each site. A typical trench might be six hundred feet long, sixty feet wide and twenty-five feet or more deep. When a trench is full it is covered with a clay cap or similar low-permeability cover and contoured for drainage and erosion control.

As stated earlier in Chapter 4, private contractors operate a number of shallow land burial facilities for the Department of Energy. Most of these facilities are adjacent to national laboratories or weapons production facilities—for example, at Oak Ridge, Tennessee, and Idaho National Engineering Laboratory in Idaho Falls, Idaho— and used for the disposal of low-level waste generated by government defense and research-and-development activities. In addition, three commercial low-level waste burial facilities now are operating—at Hanford near Richland, Washington; Beatty, Nevada; and Barnwell, South Carolina. Three former commercial sites—West Valley, New York, Maxey Flats, Kentucky, and Sheffield, Illinois— are now closed. Although no public health problem has been identified with any of these sites to date, there have been technical problems with some of them, particularly with water contamination. Many policymakers and citizens—particularly those living in areas with high rates of precipitation—are now questioning the wisdom of building additional shallow land burial facilities using traditional technology. For example, the Central Midwest Compact between Illinois and Kentucky prohibits traditional shallow land burial. The state of California is proposing to site a low-level waste facility in the desert, a location many experts consider to be ideal for shallow land burial; but even so, the state is seriously considering the construction of a facility that would include engineered barriers. At the very least is seems likely that whatever the strict technical requirements at a particular site, citizens will insist that their state take stringent technical precautions in constructing future facilities.

It should be pointed out that any new low-level waste disposal facilities must be developed under new regulations, either the Nuclear Regulatory Commission's rule (10 CFR Part 61) or, in "agreement"—that is, self-regulating—states, by equivalent state requirements. The NRC rule includes sections relating to performance objectives, technical requirements, financial assurances, licensing procedures, and state and tribal participation.

Performance objectives include provisions aimed at protecting the general population from releases of radioactivity, protecting individuals from inadvertent intrusion into the buried waste, protecting workers during operations, and ensuring the stability of the site after closure. The technical requirements for near-surface disposal include criteria for site suitability, with the primary emphasis on the long-term isolation of waste rather than short-term convenience; site design, operation, and closure; waste classification and characteristics; and, institutional requirements.

Many experts, including some who have been critical of past programs, believe that safe shallow land burial facilities can be built with careful application of the new procedures. Some critics, noting past tendencies toward technological optimism, still question whether shallow land burial is sufficiently safe.

Recently, at the request of the Nuclear Regulatory Commission, the Army Corps of Engineers undertook a study of alternative methods of low-level waste disposal including underground vaults, aboveground vaults, earth-mounded concrete bunkers, mined cavities, and augered holes. The corps study concluded that each of these methods offers some advantage over shallow land burial in meeting the performance objectives established by the Nuclear Regulatory Commission. But the design, construction, and operating costs for each of these alternatives will probably be higher and the operating procedures more complex than for shallow land burial.[11] And some experts point out that these technologies have been used only for storage and not for permanent disposal, with the exception of the earth-mounded concrete bunkers in operation in France. They cite potential drawbacks, particularly in the use of aboveground alternatives including increased worker exposure to radiation, complex operational requirements, the need for long-term maintenance and possible human intrusion.

Many observers fear that concern about past failures at shallow land burial sites may lead to the construction of unnecessarily complicated and costly alternatives to present technology. They point out that by adopting special controls for water management and incorporating natural and engineered systems, the facility at Barnwell, South Carolina, has compiled a successful record of waste containment in a humid environment.

Reduction of Low-Level Wastes

Citizens and state officials want to be certain that the amount of low-level waste—and thus any risks associated with disposal—be minimized. The combination of such public insistence, uncertainty about post-1986 disposal plans, and increasing costs for disposal at the existing commercial sites has led to heightened interest in both source reduction (reducing the amount of waste actually generated) and volume reduction (reducing the quantity of waste after it is generated). Many companies and institutions already have reduced the amount of waste they generate by changing manufacturing processes and exercising greater care in handling radioactive material and in segregating waste. Many also have reduced the volume they must ship and dispose of by increased use of compaction, incineration, filtration, and evaporation. These actions will extend the operating life of current disposal sites, limit the need for interim storage if disposal is not available, and reduce the number of shipments of low-level waste.

WHAT OTHER COUNTRIES ARE DOING

Worldwide, twenty-six countries have commercial nuclear power plants operating; nearly all have waste management programs. Although situations vary from country to country, most waste-management programs for high-level waste assume that spent fuel will be reprocessed and that the resulting high-level waste will be vitrified into glass and then disposed of in a deep geologic repository. To date, no permanent disposal of high-level waste has taken place in any country. Some countries face political opposition to siting a high-level waste repository and are therefore conducting research only on disposal alternatives or are contracting with other countries for reprocessing. Standard processes for disposal of low-level waste range from shallow land burial to sea disposal to underground disposal in played-out mines.

Cooperative International Research Programs

Eight nations—Canada, Finland, France, Japan, Sweden, Switzerland, the United Kingdom, and the United States—are currently cooperating in the International Stripa Project for high-level waste disposal. Conducted at the Stripa Mine in central Sweden under the auspices of the Organization for Economic Cooperation and Development (OECD), this research project is focused on the special characteristics of granite rock and the flow of groundwater in granite rock formations. The aim is to develop testing methods and experiments that can be used in determining the suitability of a specific site. Results are expected in 1986.

Since 1981 the United States has cooperated with the West German government in tests in the Asse II salt mine that are pertinent to the U.S. high-level waste-disposal program. The mine serves as an underground laboratory for investigation of all aspects of rock salt.

The United States also is working closely with Canada during its construction of an underground research laboratory located in a granite formation near the Whiteshell research center in Manitoba. Upon completion in 1986, the facility should make significant contributions to the two nations' ability to understand and predict the behavior of waste packages in a granite rock repository.

The Seabed Working Group, established in 1976 under the auspices of the Nuclear Energy Agency of the Organization of Economic Cooperation and Development, coordinates the various research programs of its members on the feasibility of subseabed disposal for high-level waste and low-level waste. Members include Canada, the Commission of European Communities, France, the Federal Republic of Germany, Japan, the Netherlands, Switzerland, the United Kingdom, and the United States. Belgium, Italy, and Sweden participate as observers.

Individual Waste-Management Programs

France is the only European country now operating large-scale reprocessing and vitrification facilities. The two French facilities are being expanded to handle even larger quantities of spent fuel and high-level waste. With a national commitment to plutonium-fueled fast breeder reactors and to reprocessing and recycling of spent fuel from light-water reactors, the French are actively studying the storage and disposal of transuranic waste and are also researching low-level waste disposal. France plans to store solid glass blocks of high-level waste and transuranic packages in an engineered surface facility for fifty to sixty years, then subsequently bury them at great depths in granite, salt, or clay formations. France does reprocess other countries' spent fuel and vitrifies the resultant high-level waste, but it will not dispose of other nations' wastes.

The United Kingdom now stores its high-level waste in double-wall steel tanks. A large reprocessing plant is under construction at Sellafield in northwestern England to reprocess Britain's own growing amount of spent fuel as well as fuel resulting from an increasing number of foreign contracts. The plant will vitrify the high-level waste, using a process that British experts say is simpler and less expensive than the French method. After public protests in 1981 about repository siting investigations, the United Kingdom decided to store its high-level waste indefinitely in an engineered facility and to defer decisions on a permanent repository. Britain disposed of low-level waste at sea until 1983, when seamen refused to continue hauling the waste. The British are now beginning a search for a low-level waste facility, which they plan to have operating by the early 1990s.

The Federal Republic of Germany (West Germany) has plans to build two small reprocessing plants, after the Lower Saxony state government in 1979 rejected plans to locate a reprocessing, vitrification, and disposal complex there. However, Lower Saxony will be host to several test facilities and a deep, geologic repository. This is to be located in a salt dome at Gorleben if characterization activities show the site to be suitable. At present, plans are to store spent fuel and high-level waste at an away-from-reactor facility at Gorleben and condition and store transuranic waste in surface facilities at Hanau (near Frankfurt) and Karlsruhe in southwestern Germany.

Sweden, in a national referendum in 1980, voted to complete its planned twelve-reactor construction program and then abandon nuclear power in the year 2010. Sweden does not intend to build reprocessing facilities because of expense and limited need. Instead, the government hopes to renegotiate its reprocessing contracts with France to handle all its reprocessing needs. Spent fuel and high-level waste will be stored in a shallow away-from-reactor facility excavated in crystalline granite and eventually will be disposed of in a granite repository. Low-level wastes will be disposed of in a geologic repository fifty meters under the Baltic Sea. This repository is scheduled to be completed in the 1990s.

Canada is storing spent fuel at reactors until the government makes a decision as to whether to reprocess it or until a repository is established, which will not be before 2010. With an abundant supply of natural uranium, Canada has little incentive to reprocess spent fuel. The government is building a major underground research facility at Pinawa, Manitoba, in a granite formation, and the "Waste Immobilization Process Experiment" also has been readied should Canada need to produce borosilicate glass packages to immobilize high-level waste.

India is planning for a closed nuclear fuel cycle with domestic reprocessing. However, the lack of a modern interstate road system and adequate railroads makes transport of spent fuel rods difficult; therefore, small reprocessing plants near each nuclear power plant and at-reactor storage are planned. India also is investigating potential disposal sites in geologic formations.

7

A Role for Citizens

▼　　　▼　　　▼　　　▼　　　▼

Long experience has taught that public acceptance of government decisions often hinges on conditions that are simple to state but not always easy for government to meet:

Citizens must be involved at every critical stage of the decision-making process.

The process must be reasonable, open, and accessible.

Government must give the public sufficient and understandable information about the technical and institutional aspects of a proposed program.

The process must facilitate genuine discussion among various segments of the public and the government.

If these criteria are important in deciding other controversial issues, they are doubly so in matters relating to nuclear waste.

On this issue, as on so many other public policy issues, citizens need not be experts in order to make a contribution. In fact, the nonexpert can bring valuable new perspectives to the dialogue—a longer-range view than that afforded by most elected officials, who may be looking forward to reelection in two or four years, and "human values" considerations that technical experts may underestimate.

Achieving meaningful citizen participation in a nuclear waste management program is difficult, for several reasons:

1. The technical complexity of the nuclear-waste issue discourages many citizens from participating.
2. Although citizen participation in standard-setting and licensing procedures is now required by law, most past decisions on nuclear power and waste issues were made by a small group of technical experts, some of whom continue to feel that citizens do not know enough about the issues to participate.
3. Many citizens are aware of past government failings in nuclear management and of the link between radiation exposure and cancer. Lay persons' distrust of the technical "fix" also has grown, as experts' past "fixes" have unraveled. Consequently, people may be highly skeptical and suspicious of any government effort to evaluate waste-disposal sites and guarantee public health and safety, however sound the scientific data.
4. Management and regulatory responsibilities for nuclear waste are divided. The Department of Energy has overall management responsibility for high-level waste, and the states and compacts regions manage low-level waste. Several federal agencies—the Environmental Protection Agency, the Nuclear Regulatory Commission, the Department of Transportation and the Department of the Interior—control pieces of the regulatory mosaic, and many state agencies also play a role. Thus, citizens have to become familiar with many different sets of rules for citizen participation.

Yet, despite all these obstacles, citizens have made their voices heard in the nuclear waste management debate. Working as individuals and through elected officials and public-interest and environmental organizations, many citizens have been effective in influencing state and federal policies. They have testified at congressional and regional hearings on United States high-level nuclear waste management policy and have helped shape legislation. The initial assumption of some policymakers in the low-level waste arena—that low-level waste compacts could be negotiated among officials without public review—has been successfully challenged as citizens have insisted on a significant role in state deliberations on the regional compacts. Determined citizens have found a way to be heard when decisions are made about matters that concern them or affect their lives.

Not surprisingly, public concern and attention increase as the site-selection process targets specific areas. Citizens have formed active local organizations and have become well informed about both technical and policy issues. For example, more than four hundred citizens participated in a Department of Energy briefing early in 1985 and more than forty testified at the subsequent hearing on the high-level waste environmental assessments in Hereford, Texas, a community of eighteen thousand.

However, critics of public participation still contend that it has a negative effect, citing as evidence the number of proposed projects that have been brought to a halt by citizens' actions. It is true that determined citizens have stopped proposed government actions, but it is also true that some proposals are unwise. Even though citizen action has delayed or prevented some good proposals, overall it has an impressive and growing track record for improving proposals and helping to solve difficult problems.

One of many examples from another issue area is the Cambridge Experimentation Review Board, a body of representative citizens established by the city council of Cambridge, Massachusetts. This board of "nonexperts" was able to develop proposals to govern controversial DNA research in a way that met community concerns and allowed research at Harvard University to go forward.

Well-conceived, properly funded public participation in nuclear waste management can lead to a number of highly desirable results, such as a well-informed citizenry, a decision-making process that citizens know to be open to public inspection and responsive to public concerns, improved waste-management decisions benefiting from broad public input and review, and enhanced citizen cooperation in the implementation of decisions considered to be scientifically sound and publicly acceptable.

THE PUBLIC'S ROLE IN HIGH-LEVEL WASTE MANAGEMENT

Congress was explicit in the Nuclear Waste Policy Act about the importance of public participation in decision-making on high-level waste. The act states that "State and public participation in planning and development of repositories is essential in order to promote public confidence in the safety of disposal of such waste and spent fuel." However, whereas the act cites many specific *requirements* for state and tribal participation, the *opportunities* for public participation are not so clearly spelled out.

Encouraged by citizens and other levels of government, the Department of Energy has recognized the necessity of fleshing out this bare-bones outline. The agency chose to hold hearings on the siting guidelines and to sponsor a series of public briefings and hearings on the environmental assessments for the proposed first repository sites.

Nevertheless, the high-level waste program does raise some formidable barriers to participation—particularly because of its highly technical content, by the size of the project, and by the amount of time that is bound to elapse between major decision points. Undoubtedly, however, effective participation in the process for any individual or group will be based on the traditional foundations of effective political action: staying informed about the issues and about timetables, finding allies, understanding the particular contribution one can make to solving the problem, planning strategy, expressing one's views at a time when they can make a difference, holding officials accountable for the decisions they make. Of course, every citizen will not be able to participate at all times and in all ways, but whatever the limits of time or resources, a way should be open for each to be heard.

What Citizens Can Do

To Stay Informed About the Issue as a Whole Begin with additional background reading. Ask your local library to get some of the references listed in Resources.

Ask to be on the mailing list for the *Office of Civilian Radioactive Waste Management Bulletin*, a monthly publication, by writing to OCRWM, U.S. Department of Energy, 1000 Independence Ave. S.W., Washington D.C. 20585.

Ask to be on the mailing list of the agency responsible for your major concern: the Department of Transportation, the Environmental Protection Agency, the Nuclear Regulatory Commission, the Department of Energy. (See Resources, p 83.)

Monitor the *Federal Register*, which contains notices of executive branch and regulatory agency meetings and rulemakings, proposed regulations, information on hearings, comment periods, contacts for additional information, final regulations and effective dates. The *Register* is published daily and is available from libraries and from the United States Government Printing Office.

Contact your members of Congress and ask to be kept informed about pending legislation or hearings.

Join an organization that monitors and reports on developments in high-level waste management.

Visit or contact Department of Energy regional offices, reading rooms, or information offices located near potential repository sites. (See Resources, p. 83)

To Influence the Development of the Program   If your state is being evaluated as a possible site for a high-level or spent-fuel facility:

1. Monitor the development of the Department of Energy's funding agreements with your state to be certain that adequate provision is made for public involvement.
2. Learn what funds are available (for example, state or Department of Energy grants to support local involvement and independent scientific review). Work to see that these resources are used effectively.
3. Find out which state officials are responsible for technical and policy review of the Department of Energy's proposals. Make sure that the state provides enough time and expertise for the job to be done well.
4. Organize or encourage local programs presenting general information on such subjects as the nature of radiation or the scientific/technical basis for the development of repositories. Ask your local library to obtain background information. When people become more familiar with the issues, their confidence and effectiveness increase.
5. Learn how to be effective in responding to federal proposals. A number of handbooks and workshops can be helpful.
6. Respond to opportunities to comment orally or in writing on state or federal proposals.
7. Join a local or national organization that shares your interests—or form a group to help you with the study, analysis, and monitoring that will lead to effective participation.

8. Promote media coverage of the issues. Write letters to the editor.

PUBLIC INVOLVEMENT IN LOW-LEVEL WASTE MANAGEMENT

There are four levels of government acting in low-level waste issues: federal (especially Congress), compact regions, states, and potential host communities. Each has some responsibility for policy and for regulation.

As was discussed in Chapter 5, regional compacts must be submitted to Congress for approval. In reviewing the proposed compacts, Congress has been considering the impact of regional groupings on a national system of low-level waste disposal. Congress also must resolve the problem of keeping the commitments made in its own Low-Level Radioactive Waste Policy Act of 1980 to current host states—relieving them of the total burden for national disposal on January 1, 1986—while ensuring that disposal or storage options will be available to other states between that deadline and the time when additional facilities are ready to take the waste.

Meanwhile, regional compact commissions are considering management systems and regulations. Those that do not have disposal sites are also deciding how and where to site new facilities. States that may be chosen to build a regional facility are developing the necessary siting processes and regulations. States that do not yet belong to compacts are making more fundamental decisions about how to meet their responsibility under the law. In most cases, potential host communities have not been identified. The local level will be part of the action later.

What Citizens Can Do

First, get the facts. Find out what the situation is in your state and/or region, and then decide whether to become involved in specific regional, state, or local issues or in national policy questions.

At the State Level

1. Find out what type and how much low-level waste is produced in your state, who is producing it, and how it is cur-

rently being disposed of. Publications from the National Low-Level Waste Program of EG&G Idaho (see Resources) are a good starting point.

2. Contact your state representative or state senator to learn the status of compacts or other state low-level radioactive waste legislation.

3. Find out which state agencies are responsible for policy implementation and for regulation and whether the state is an agreement (self-regulating) state. Ask to be on mailing lists for information or meeting notices.

4. If your state belongs to a compact region, identify your state's representatives to the compact commission. Find out whether decisions have been made about new facilities. Ask to be on the compact authority's mailing list for meeting notices and summaries.

5. Find out what area or local organizations or individuals have been following the issue and ask them for an update.

Once you know what stage low-level waste management has reached in your state, you can decide at what level and to what extent you wish to be involved with the remaining decision process. You can:

1. Join or form a group to monitor the development of a low-level waste-management system for your state and region.

2. Review the state or compact region plans for public information and involvement programs. If they are inadequate, work for improvements.

3. Respond to opportunities for comment on proposals, in writing or in person at workshops or hearings.

4. Let state and local officials know of your interest and your specific concerns.

At the National Level

1. Contact your members of Congress and let them know you are interested in the issue. Find out the status of compact approval and any proposed amendments to the Low-Level Radioactive Waste Policy Act of 1980. Ask to be informed about any hearings or other opportunities to be involved in national policy development.

2. Put your name on the mailing lists for low-level waste issues handled by the Environmental Protection Agency, the Department of Transportation, the Nuclear Regulatory Commission, and the Department of Energy. (see Resources, p. 83)
3. Join national organizations monitoring the issue and be certain you receive their newsletters.
4. Make known your opinions about proposed legislation or regulations directly to the officials responsible. Comment at public meetings and hearings. Write letters to the editor of local or state newspapers.

CONCLUSIONS

The construction of any facility for the disposal or storage of radioactive waste will have an immediate impact on the citizens of neighboring communities. Moreover, the potential exists for harm to public health and the environment—over the short term, during development, operation, and transportation to a facility, and over the long-term period while the waste remains hazardous. Decisions about such facilities must be made carefully and deliberately to ensure that disruption of affected communities, risk to public health, and likelihood of environmental degradation are acceptably low.

Some citizens will follow the decision and implementation process diligently during all its phases. Others will become involved only at major decision points or when a potential decision affects them directly. Citizens can play their important roles well only if they have accurate, understandable, timely information, sufficient time and technical support, and an opportunity to be heard. Citizens can work to ensure that the agencies responsible provide these tools, and then they must prepare to use them wisely.

Citizens will need to remember that the wheels of government turn slowly and that many nuclear waste management decisions will take years to fully evolve. But by getting involved, citizens can help shape the ground rules—the key management plans, strategies, and regulations—and thus help ensure effective and equitable policies in the future.

Notes

▼   ▼   ▼   ▼   ▼

1. Committee on the Biological Effects of Ionizing Radiations, *The Effects on Population of Exposure to Low Levels of Ionizing Radiation: 1980* (Washington, D.C.: National Academy Press, 1980), p. 2.
2. Ibid., p. iii.
3. *Spent Fuel Storage Requirements, DOE/RL 83-1,* January 1983.
4. D.G. Jacobs, J.S. Epler, and R.R. Rose, *Identification of Technical Problems Encountered in Shallow Land Burial of Low-Level Radioactive Wastes,* Oak Ridge, Tennessee: Evaluation Research Corporation, ORNL/SUB-80/13619/1.
5. DOE/LLW-27T, EG&G Idaho Inc.
6. R. Dale Smith, Harry J. Pettengill, and Edward F. Hawkins, *Recent Developments in Uranium Mill Regulations and the Status of the Uranium Milling Industry,* February 1985.
7. Environmental Policy Institute, *Safety Problems with Nuclear Transportation,* Washington, D.C., June 21, 1985.
8. Office of Technology Assessment, U.S. Congress, *Managing the Nation's Commercial High-Level Radioactive Waste* (Washington, D.C., March 1985).
9. Waste Isolation Systems Panel, Board on Radioactive Waste Management, *A Study of the Isolation System for Geologic Disposal of Radioactive Wastes* (Washington, D.C.: National Academy of Sciences, 1983).
10. Panel on Waste Isolation Pilot Plant, Board on Radioactive Waste Management, *Review of the Scientific and Technical Criteria for Waste Isolation Pilot Plant (WIPP)* (Washington, D.C.: National Academy of Sciences, 1984).
11. *Alternative Methods for Disposal of Low-Level Radioactive Waste,* NUREG/CR3774, vol 1.

Resources

▼   ▼   ▼   ▼   ▼

ORGANIZATIONS

Government Agencies

U.S. Department of Energy
Office of Civilian Radioactive Waste Management, Department of Energy, 1000 Independence Avenue, S.W., Washington, DC 20585.
Nuclear Regulatory Commission, Division of Waste Management, Office of Nuclear Material Safety & Standards, 1717 H Street, N.W., Washington, DC 20555.
Office of Technology Assessment, U.S. Congress, Washington, DC 20510.
U.S. Department of Interior. Geologic Survey Public Inquiries, 1028 General Services Administration Office, 19th & F Streets, N.W., Washington, DC 20244. Bureau of Land Management, 18th and C Sts., N.W., Washington, DC 20240.
U.S. Department of Transportation, Research & Special Programs Administration, Office of Hazardous Materials Regulations, Materials Transportation Bureau, 400 7th Street, S.W., Washington, DC 20590.
U.S. Environmental Protection Agency, Office of Radiation Programs, 401 M Street, S.W., Washington, DC 20460.

Nongovernmental Agencies

American Nuclear Energy Council, 410 First Street, S.E., Washington, DC 20003.
Atomic Industrial Forum, Inc., 7101 Wisconsin Avenue, Bethesda, MD 20814.

Battelle Memorial Institute, 505 King Avenue, Columbus, OH 43201.

Environmental Policy Institute, 218 D Street, S.E., Washington, DC 20003.

National Conference of State Legislatures, 1405 Curtis Street, 23rd Floor, Denver, CO 80202.

National Governors' Association, 444 North Capitol Street, Suite 250, Washington, DC 20001.

National Low-Level Waste Management Program, EG&G, Idaho, Inc., P.O. Box 1625, Idaho Falls, ID 83415.

Natural Resource Defense Council, 1350 New York Ave., N.W., Washington, DC 20005.

Nuclear Information and Resource Service, 1346 Connecticut Ave., N.W., Washington, DC 20036.

Sierra Club Radioactive Waste Campaign, 78 Elwood Street, Buffalo, NY 14201.

Southwest Research and Information Center, P.O. Box 4524, Albuquerque, NM 87106.

Union of Concerned Scientists, 1346 Connecticut Avenue, N.W., Washington, DC 20036.

U.S. Committee for Energy Awareness, 1735 I Street, N.W., Suite 500, Washington, DC 20006.

Utility Nuclear Waste Management Group, 1111 19th Street, N.W., Washington, DC 20036-3691.

PUBLICATIONS

Alternative Methods for Disposal of Low-Level Radioactive Wastes: Task 1: Description of Methods and Assessment of Criteria. Prepared for U.S. Nuclear Regulatory Commission. 1984. 84pp. $4.50. Order from Superintendent of Documents, U.S. Government Printing Office, Washington, DC 20402, GPO No. NUREG/CR-3774.

Atoms to Electricity. Assistant Secretary for Nuclear Energy, Office of Support Programs, U.S. Department of Energy. DOE/NE-0053. 1983. 68pp. Free. Order from ENERGY-DOE, P.O. Box 62, Oak Ridge, TN 37830.

The Citizen's Nuclear Waste Manual. Laura D. Worby. Nuclear Information and Resource Service, 1346 Connecticut Avenue, N.W., Washington, DC 20036. 1984. 150pp. $20.

Disposing of Low-Level Radioactive Waste in California. League of Women Voters Southern California Regional Task Force. 1984. 28pp. $2.00. Order from LWV of California, 926 J Street, Suite 1000, Sacramento, CA 95814.

Effects on Populations of Exposure to Low Levels of Ionizing Radiation: 1980. The Committee on the Biological Effects of Ionizing Radiations (BEIR), Division of Medical Sciences, Assembly of Life Sciences, National Research Council. 1980. 540pp. $18. Order from the National Academy Press, 2101 Constitution Avenue, N.W., Washington, DC 20418.

Low-Level Radioactive Waste Management: An Update. National Conference of State Legislatures. 1984. 80pp. $7.50.

Low-Level Radioactive Waste Policy Act Report, Response to Public Law 96-573. DE81027680/LA. $10 + $3 handling. Order from National Technical Information Service, 5285 Port Royal Road, Springfield, VA 22161. 1981.

Managing the Nation's Commercial High-Level Radioactive Waste. Office of Technology Assessment. Full report available from Superintendent of Documents, U.S. Government Printing Office, Washington, DC 20402, GPO Stock No. 052-003-00980-3. 1985. $9.50. Report summary available free from OTA, reference no. OTA-0-277.

Methods to Decrease Low-Level Waste Generation. Low-Level Radioactive Waste Management Handbook Series. Pacific Northwest Laboratory, Battelle Memorial Institute. 1982.

Mission Plan for the Civilian Radioactive Waste Management Program (draft). Two volumes. Office of Civilian Radioactive Waste Management, U.S. Department of Energy. 1984. Free. DOE/RW-0005 DRAFT available from Office of Public Affairs, Draft Mission Plan for Radioactive Waste, U.S. Department of Energy, Room 1E-218, Forrestal Building, 1000 Independence Avenue, S.W., Washington, DC 20585.

Nuclear Power in America's Future. Atomic Industrial Forum. 1984. 20pp. 1 copy free.

Nuclear Waste Disposal: Closing the Circle. Dr. George Russ, Atomic Industrial Forum. 1984. 26pp. $3.00. The Atomic Industrial Forum will issue a publication on low-level waste in late 1985.

Planner's Guide to Low-Level Radioactive Waste Disposal, A. Thomas P. Smith. American Planning Association, 1313 E. 60th St., Chicago, IL 60637, Planning Advisory Service Report #369. 1982. 53pp. $6.

Process for Locating Shallow Land Burial Sites for Low-Level Radioactive Waste, A. DOE/LLW-16T. Oak Ridge National Labaoratory and EG&G Idaho, Inc. Available from National Low-Level Waste Management Program, Idaho EG&G. 1983. (See nongovernmental agencies.)

Radioactive Exchange, The. Edward L. Helminski, publisher, P.O. Box 9528, Washington, DC 20016. 20 issues per year subscription for $279.

Radioactive Waste Management. Merril Eisenbud, New York University Medical Center. Reprinted from *Outlook for Science and Technology: The Next Five Years.* National Research Council. San Francisco: W. H. Freeman and Company. 1982. pp.286–820.

Radioactive Waste: Politics, Technology and Risk. Ronnie D. Lipshutz. Union of Concerned Scientists. 1980. 225pp.

"Radioactivity and You." Merril Eisenbud. *Environment*, vol. 26, No. 10. December 1984.

Regional Low-Level Radioactive Waste Disposal Sites—Progress Being Made but New Sites Will Probably Not Be Ready by 1986. General Accounting Office. April 11, 1983. 66pp. Free. Report #GAO/RCED-83-48 available from U.S. General Accounting Office, Document Handling and Information Services Facility, P.O. Box 6015, Gaithersburg, MD 20760.

Spent Fuel and Radioactive Waste Inventories, Projections, and Characteristics. Oak Ridge National Laboratory for U.S. Department of Energy, Assistant Secretary for Nuclear Energy and Assistant Secretary for Defense Programs. 1983. 300pp. Order DOE/NE-0017/2 from National Technical Information Service, U.S. Department of Commerce, Springfield, VA 22161.

Study of the Isolation System for Geologic Disposal of Radioactive Wastes, A. Waste Isolation Systems Panel, Board on Radioactive Waste Management, Commission on Physical Sciences, Mathematics, and Resources, National Research Council. 1983. Available from the National Academy Press, 2101 Constitution Avenue, NW, Washington, DC 20418.

Understanding Radioactive Waste. 2nd ed. Raymond L. Murray. 1983. 120pp. $10. Order from Battelle Press, Battelle Memorial Institute.

Workbook: The Nuclear Legacy—How Safe Is It? The. vol VII, nos. 4 & 5, July–October 1983. Southwest Research and Information Center. 1983. 24pp. $1.00.

Glossary

▼   ▼   ▼   ▼   ▼

activation products. Atomic fragments absorbed by the steel of the reactor vessel or by minerals in the water used for cooling that give off radiation for years.

activity. The rate at which radioactive material emits radiation, stated in terms of the number of nuclear disintegrations occurring in a unit of time; the common unit of radioactivity is the curie (Ci).

agreement state. A state that has entered into an agreement with the Nuclear Regulatory Commission to assume regulatory responsibility for radioactive materials under Section 274 of the Atomic Energy Act of 1954 as amended.

alpha particle. Positively charged particle emitted by certain radioactive material, made up of two neutrons and two protons. It cannot penetrate clothing or the outer layer of skin.

atom. The basic component of all matter; it is the smallest part of an element having all the chemical properties of that element. Atoms are made up of protons and neutrons (in the nucleus) and electrons.

atomic mass. The number of protons and neutrons in an atom. For instance, uranium-238 has an atomic mass of 238—92 protons and 146 neutrons.

backfill. The material used to fill in around casks after they have been placed in a repository or shallow land burial trench.

backfilling. Another layer of protection to prevent radioactive material from entering the environment.

background radiation. Radiation arising from natural radioactive materials always present in the environment, including solar and cosmic radiation and radioactive elements in the upper atmosphere, the ground, building materials, and the human body.

basalt. An igneous rock of volcanic origin, usually fine-grained and black or dark gray.

bedded. Layered deposit of sediment in the form of rocks, products of weathering, organic materials, and precipitates.

beta particle. A negatively charged particle emitted in the radioactive decay of certain nuclides. A beta particle has mass and charge equal to that of an electron and has a short range in air and low ability to penetrate other materials.

boiling water reactor. A light-water–cooled reactor in which the water coolant that passes through the reactor is converted to high-pressure steam that flows through the turbine.

breeder reactor. A reactor that produces more FISSILE material than it consumes (by a process called "breeding").

canister. The outermost container into which glassified high-level waste or spent fuel rods are to be placed. Made of stainless steel or an inert alloy.

cask. Container that provides shielding during transportation of canisters of radioactive materials. Usually measures 12 feet in diameter by 22 feet long and weighs 200 tons.

chain reaction. (controlled) A self-sustaining series of nuclear fissions taking place in a reactor core. Neutrons produced in one fission cause the next fission.

cladding. Protective alloy shielding in which fissionable fuel is inserted. Cladding is relatively resistant to radiation and to the physical and chemical conditions in a reactor core. The cladding may be of stainless steel or some alloy such as zircalloy.

commercial wastes. Low-level and high-level (including spent fuel) radioactive wastes generated by commercial nuclear power plants, manufacturing industries, and institutions (hospitals, universities, research institutions).

curie. A measure of the rate of radioactive decay; it is equivalent to the radioactivity of one gram of radium or 37 billion disintegrations per second. A nanocurie is one billionth of a curie; a picocurie is one trillionth of a curie.

daughter product. Nuclides resulting from the radioactive decay of other nuclides. A daughter product may be either stable or radioactive.

decay. Disintegration of the nucleus of an unstable nuclide by spontaneous emission of charged particles, photons, or both.

decontamination. The removal of radioactive material from the surface or from within another material.

defense wastes. Radioactive waste resulting from weapons research and development, the operation of naval reactors, the production of weapons materials, the reprocessing of defense spent fuel, and the decommissioning of nuclear-powered ships and submarines.

disposal. Permanent removal from man's environment with no provision for continuous human control and maintenance.

dome. A bed that arches up to form a rounded peak deposit, e.g., a salt dome.

dose. Quantity of radiation or energy absorbed; measured in RADS.

exposure. A measure of ionization produced in air by X rays or by GAMMA RADIATION. Acute exposure generally refers to a high level of exposure of short duration; chronic exposure is lower-level exposure of long duration.

fissile. Able to be split by a low-energy neutron, for example, U-235.

fission. The splitting or breaking apart of a heavy atom such as uranium. When a uranium atom is split, large amounts of energy and one or more neutrons are released.

fission products. A general term for the complex mixture of nuclides produced as a result of nuclear fission. Most, but not all, nuclides in the mixture are radioactive and they decay, forming additional (daughter) products, with the result that the complex mixture of fission products so formed contains about 200 different isotopes of over 35 elements.

fuel cycle. The complete series of steps involved in supplying fuel for nuclear reactors. It includes mining, refining, the original fabrication of fuel elements, their use in a reactor, and management of spent fuel and radioactive wastes. A closed fuel cycle includes chemical reprocessing to recover the fissionable material remaining in the spent fuel; an open fuel cycle does not.

gamma radiation. Short-wavelength electromagnetic radiation emitted in the radioactive decay of certain nuclides. Gamma rays are highly penetrating.

geologic isolation. The disposal of radioactive wastes deep beneath the earth's surface.

half-life. Time required for a radioactive substance to lose 50 percent of its activity by decay. The half-life of the radioisotope plutonium-239, for example, is about 24,000 years. Starting with a pound of plutonium-239, in 24,000 years there will be ½ pound of plutonium-239, in another 24,000 years there will be ¼ pound and so on. (A pound of actual material remains but it gradually becomes a stable element.)

high-level waste (HLW). Highly radioactive material, containing FISSION PRODUCTS, traces of uranium and plutonium, and other TRANSURANIC elements, that results from chemical reprocessing of SPENT FUEL. Originally produced in liquid form, HLW must be solidified before disposal.

igneous. Formed by solidification of molten rock.

interim storage. The temporary holding of wastes on or away from the generator's site when disposal space is not available. Monitoring and human control are provided, and subsequent action involving treatment, transportation, or final disposition is expected.

ion. Atomic particle, atom, or chemical radical bearing an electric charge, either negative or positive.

ion exchange. A chemical process involving the reversible interchange of various ions between a solution and a solid material. It is used to separate and purify chemicals, such as FISSION PRODUCTS or rare earths in solution. This process also takes place with many minerals found in nature and with ions in solution such as groundwater.

ionization. Removal of electrons from an atom, for example, by means of radiation, so that the atom becomes charged.

ionizing radiation. Types of radiation capable of removing one or more electrons from atoms they encounter, leaving positively charged particles such as alpha and beta, and nonparticulate forms such as X rays and gamma radiation. High enough doses of ionizing radiation may cause cellular damage. Nonionizing radiation includes visible, ultraviolet, and infrared light as well as radio waves.

isotopes. Different forms of the same chemical element, which are distinguished by having different numbers of neutrons (but the same number of protons) in the nucleus of their atoms. A single element may have many isotopes. For example, uranium appears in nature in three forms: uranium-234 (142 neutrons), uranium-235 (143 neutrons), and uranium-238 (148 neutrons); each uranium isotope has 92 protons.

latent period. The period or state of seeming inactivity between the time of exposure of tissue to an acute radiation dose and the onset of the final stage of radiation sickness.

light-water reactor (LWR). A nuclear reactor cooled and moderated by water.

linear hypothesis. The assumption that any radiation causes biological damage, according to a straight-line graph of health effect versus dose.

low-level waste (LLW). Radioactive waste not classified as high-level waste, transuranic waste, spent fuel, or byproduct material. Most are generally short-lived and have low radioactivity.

mobility. The ability of radionuclides to move through food chains in the environment.

neutron. Uncharged particle in a nucleus. Neutrons are used to split heavy atoms in the fission reaction.

pressurized water reactor (PWR). A light-water–cooled reactor operated at high pressure without boiling.

rad (radiation absorbed dose). The amount, or dose, of ionizing radiation absorbed by any material, such as human tissue.

radiation. Particles or waves from atomic or nuclear processes (or from certain machines). Prolonged exposure to these particles and rays may be harmful.

radioactive. Of, caused by, or exhibiting radioactivity.

radioactivity. The spontaneous emission of radiation from the nucleus of an atom. Radioisotopes of elements lose particles and energy through this process of radioactive decay.

radioisotope. An unstable isotope of an element that will eventually undergo radioactive decay (i.e., disintegration).

radionuclide. A radioactive species of an atom characterized by the constitution of its nucleus; in nuclear medicine, an atomic species emitting ionizing radiation and capable of existing for a measurable time, so that it may be used to image organs and tissues.

radon. A radioactive gas that is produced by the decay of one of the daughters of radium. Radon is hazardous in unventilated areas because it can build up to high concentrations and, if inhaled for long periods of time, may induce lung cancer.

rem (roentgen equivalent man). Unit used in radiation protection to measure the amount of damage to human tissue from a dose of ionizing radiation.

repository. A permanent disposal facility for high-level or transuranic wastes and spent fuel.

reprocessing. The process by which spent fuel is separated into waste material for disposal and material such as uranium and plutonium, to be reused.

resin. A synthetic material used for ion exchange or a high-molecular-weight organic material (i.e., glue, epoxy) used to solidify liquid materials.

scintillation liquids. Organic chemical solutions that produce light when bombarded with radiation. These liquids are a major component of institutional low-level wastes.

shale. Compacted clay rock.

shielding. Materials, usually concrete, water, and lead, placed around radioactive materials to protect personnel against the danger of radiation.

source term. The amount and type of radioactive material released into the environment in the case of a severe nuclear accident.

spent fuel. Fuel that has been "burned" (irradiated) in a nuclear power plant's reactor to the point where it no longer contributes efficiently to the nuclear chain reaction. Spent fuel is thermally hot and highly radioactive.

storage. Operations that are designed to provide isolation and easy recovery of radioactive materials, and which rely on continuous human monitoring maintenance and protection from human intrusion for a specified period of time.

threshold hypothesis. A radiation-dose-consequence hypothesis that holds that biological radiation effects will occur only above some minimum dose.

transuranic waste (TRU). Waste materials contaminated with U-233 (and its daughter products), certain isotopes of plutonium, and nuclides with atomic number greater than 92 (uranium). It is produced primarily from reprocessing spent fuel and from use of plutonium in fabrication of nuclear weapons.

tuff. A rock composed of compacted volcanic ash and dust; it is usually porous and soft.

volume reduction. Various methods of waste treatment, such as evaporation for liquids or compaction for solids, aimed at reducing the volume of waste.